James O Evans

THE WALTER LYNWOOD FLEMING
LECTURES IN SOUTHERN HISTORY

LOUISIANA STATE UNIVERSITY

OTHER PUBLISHED LECTURES IN THE SERIES:

THE
RURAL PRESS
AND THE
NEW SOUTH

By

THOMAS D. CLARK

Published by LOUISIANA

STATE UNIVERSITY PRESS

Baton Rouge

To

A. L. BENNETT

IN APPRECIATION FOR HIS
THOUGHTFULNESS OF ME

INTRODUCTION

THE three lectures contained in this brief study
of the southern weekly press attempt to present as
many phases of the institution. These chapters are
organized from the viewpoint that they best illus-
trate the role of the country paper in the life of the
common man in the South. Editors grew more numerous after 1870, and between 1880 and 1910 the
weekly field in the South became rather adequately
developed. Taking advantage of new mechanical de-
vices for printing, and improved news facilities for
widening the horizon of the papers, southern weekly
editors increased their subscription lists and the influence of their papers. As a result of these changes
the papers assumed an ever-growing social, economic, and political influence in their respective
communities. To them the New South was extremely real, and they campaigned vigorously for
some of the industrial advantages offered by the
new era in American economic life.

Editors were equally aware of regional failures.
Social institutions floundered on the rocks of antiquity
and inefficiency, and the papers shouted demands for

improvements. Friction developed between the races, and the better-informed portion of the press begged for calm and orderly adjustment. Lynching, public hanging, and crime stimulated many a pen to flow with eloquent appeals for a correction of sectional evils. Crises in agriculture and business required more than ordinary editorial foresight in heading off calamity for the common people. The boll weevil, the Texas tick, and the hookworm were three ogres which hovered menacingly above editorial desks and threatened large blocks of subscribers with economic extinction. Bad roads, weed-grown streets, broken pavements, filthy public wells, run-down jails and courthouses, dilapidated pesthouses and poorhouses, abuse of convicts by private lessors, poor officials, and other issues furnished grist to the editorial mill. Education was ever an important progeny of the editorial mind, and the press labored consistently for better schools.

On the lighter side of rural life, papers carried endless columns of local and homely news, stories of backwoodsmen in embarrassing but comic situations, and impossible folk stories of death and calamity, of ghosts and earth rumblings. In fact, the fading pages of the files of country papers tell a most human story of the South. Buried here and awaiting the coming industrious ghouls of formal history lie many intimate explanations of why Southerners have always behaved as they do. Here are the innermost stories of how the South reknitted itself into the Union with both big and little sinews of human *rapprochement* in an effort to heal the tear caused by war, and to erase the nauseating purplish scars of sectional discord.

These chapters touch on all of these phases of southern life, but in a restricted way; my more extensive study covers the subject in more detail. Here I have endeavored to distill as carefully as possible the essence of one of the South's most human and useful institutions—the country weekly.

THOMAS D. CLARK

Lexington, Kentucky
July 22, 1947

CONTENTS

[xi]

I

THE PEOPLE'S PRESS

IN 1874 an ink-stained Georgia country editor
dreamed that he had died and was standing just outside the Pearly Gates when he was greeted from
within by a loud, hysterical outcry. This noise came
from a group of former subscribers who asked most
embarrassing questions in this moment of his entrance
upon the celestial life. One wanted to know what the
editor had done with the curious egg which he had
left in the newspaper office. Another cried, "Where's
the piece you promised to write about my new soda
fountain?" A familiar voice asked why Old Peddle's
new picket fence attracted so much attention while
his went unnoticed. Above all this medley of angelic
protestation rose the painful demand as to why one
outraged soul's name had been misspelled. A female
seraph wanted an explanation as to why the account
of her wedding had been recorded among the death notices. A David Harum in a southern accent demanded
an explanation as to why the editor had written such
a sensational story about a runaway scrape in which

the reputation of his horse was completely ruined for trading purposes. The village poetess was there, and in a petulant whimper she accused the poor old editor of having botched her verse. A tedious literary companion was most embarrassing of all because he demanded the return of his manuscript. Thus, standing on the very threshold of a glorious eternity, the old Georgian was reminded of many of the reasons for publishing a country paper, and of most of the local editorial sins.

When the Civil War ended, many editors, who had ceased business either to serve in the army or because their print shops were destroyed by military raids, began the republication of their papers. Many of these papers appeared on one sheet which carried a limited amount of news and an equally meager quantity of advertising. Surprisingly, there were advertisements of consumer goods in these first issues, and there was some evidence that business in areas of the South was being renewed with success. Added to this list of papers were a few which had continued publication throughout the war. Their routine was not interrupted by its cessation.

In these early postwar years, the editorial field was regarded as a highly desirable profession in which a young man with limited resources might embark with success. Like storekeeping and other trades open to men who previously had gone into one of the more formal professions, the weekly-newspaper field offered respectable employment, a chance to speak out against the outrages of Reconstruction, some immediate income, and considerable promise for the future.

No great amount of formal education was necessary to edit the average weekly paper. An ability to read, to write, and to use plenty of horse sense; personal courage; and the facility to work with one's hands seem to have been the main requirements. Few if any of the editors went to college, many never attended high school, but all of them voiced a respect for education, despite the fact that country newspaper offices housed the biggest collection of self-made men to be found in the South. It is impossible to make more than a cursory mention of the names of a very few of the men who became influential in their communities because of their editorial positions. Among these were Sidney Lewis of the Sparta (Georgia) *Ishmaelite,* Will C. Hight of the *Winston County* (Mississippi) *Journal,* B. C. Knapp of the Fayette (Mississippi) *Chronicle,* W. P. and Ed Walton of the Stanford (Kentucky) *Interior Journal,* Dan M. Bowmar of the Woodford (Kentucky) *Sun,* Lewis M. Grist of the Yorkville (South Carolina) *Enquirer,* E. H. Aull of the Newberry (South Carolina) *Herald and News,* H. A. London of the Chatham (North Carolina) *Record,* L. W. McCord of the Pulaski (Tennessee) *Citizen,* S. A. Jonas of the Aberdeen (Mississippi) *Examiner,* W. D. Jelks of

[3]

the Eufaula (Alabama) *Times and News,* and W. B. Townsend of the Dahlonega (Georgia) *Nugget.* Every one of these men was strong-willed, determined, and full of the courage of his convictions, and was an active influence in the social and political affairs of his home community.

Just as a limited amount of formal education was sufficient to conduct a paper editorially, it was likewise possible to begin the publication of a weekly with limited mechanical facilities. A small stock of type, a printer's stone, four iron chases, an inking pan and roller, a couple of crude tables, a filthy towel, and a Washington or Franklin hand press were all the equipment necessary. Actually, little basic mechanical change was made in the small printing shop from the day of John Gutenberg until the late 1870's and 1880's when the Meihle, "Country" Campbell, and Babcock flatbed presses were put into general use. It was not until the second decade of this century that linotype machines were much used in country printing offices. Little highly developed technical skill was necessary to do a fair job of "sticking" type. It was not only possible, but true in many cases that one man edited, composed, and printed a paper. Many editors took a short cut by composing and setting news items and editorials directly from their type cases without writing them on a piece of paper. If pulling the lever of an old-type Washington press was too difficult for the editor, he could always hire a husky Negro to perform the task for him, and a devil to ink the forms. No expensive building was required to house the simple plant, and the farther from the main loafing centers of the town it was located the better. Nevertheless, a newspaper office was as attractive for whiling away time as a country store, and loafers were ever-present to pass on the news and to fray the nerves of typesetters.

Within a decade after the war, southern publishers found relief from their burdens of writing and composing type for their papers. Far removed from the southern scene, in Berlin, Wisconsin, the first newspaper auxiliary service was begun in 1861 as an exigency of war. David Atwood and Horace Rublee made a practical application of an old idea to a new principle of publishing. They supplied to local papers in their area ready-printed official matter which went into their Wisconsin *State Journal*. Soon after the war the auxiliary service was expanded to include both boiler plate and readyprint. Boiler plate was a single column of printed matter which could be used at will throughout the make-up of a paper, and was impressed on thin metal castings mounted on special "type high" foundations so as to permit its use on standard chases. Readyprint was printed pages of paper stock, usually undated and without title heads to permit its use with any weekly of a given size. This service was delivered weekly at a nominal annual cost. From the beginning, the idea took hold generally. At

Chicago, Ansel Nash Kellogg, often called the father of the newspaper syndicate, began supplying ready-print for the midwestern papers in 1866, and by the time of the disastrous fire of October, 1871, he had built up a large clientele. The fire destroyed his paper stock, equipment, and subscription lists, but soon after the calamity he purchased new materials in the East and was back in business. The auxiliary services grew by leaps and bounds. Branch offices were established in nearly every thickly settled area in the United States. Within a short space of time these organizations were consolidated into newspaper unions, most of which were eventually acquired by the powerful Western Newspaper Union and formed into a near monopoly which exerted a wide influence in the country-paper field. In the South, readyprint and boiler plate were distributed from central offices located in Nashville, Memphis, Vicksburg, New Orleans, Birmingham, Atlanta, Charlotte, Baltimore, and Cincinnati.

As interesting as the corporate and mechanical history of the auxiliary services is, it does not overshadow their literary aspects. To the country reader these services supplied a much more varied selection of reading material than otherwise could have been possible. Back of the local publisher was a highly trained and "sectionally aware" staff of editors who prepared copy to be distributed each week. A large portion of the matter published was of an "ever-green" nature. That is, a man lying abed in a dingy Alabama or Georgia cabin might spot on the newspaper-covered ceiling of the room a story published ten years before which was as timely in interest as it was the day it was printed. There were political and religious features, practical, mechanical, and agricultural hints, moral fictional stories, pictures of the world's wondrous things, patriotic material, and, always, columns of dull humor. Great care was used not to publish in the South any political or religious stories which would incur the wrath of a conservative southern Protestant Democrat. Apparently most of the news services took the extreme precaution not to err in these matters, and extracted controversial materials from southern dailies such as the *Courier-Journal*, the Richmond *Times-Dispatch*, the Memphis *Commercial-Appeal* and *Scimitar*, the New Orleans *Times-Picayune*, the Atlanta *Constitution*, the Augusta *Chronicle*, the Charlotte *Observer*, and the Charleston *News and Courier*.

From a strictly modern viewpoint, use of ready-print might indicate an unprogressive paper which was published either by a lazy and indifferent editor, or by one who was wholly without imagination and mechanical equipment necessary to fill up four blank pages of paper each week. However, looked at from the vantage point of southern newspaper history, the auxiliary services made the establishment and continued publication of hundreds of southern weeklies a possibility.

The local southern newspapers themselves were great public news and opinion outlets for their communities. Actually they constituted tiny but powerful drops of enlightenment which pecked away incessantly at the great stone barriers of regional isolation and provincialism. These papers brought some news and special-feature stories in from the outside world, and often rolled back the invisible curtain of silence and expanded to a much wider perimeter the horizon of public knowledge and interest. Inside the locality of a paper almost every problem that could confront a community was publicized and discussed. Common men who wished to be heard beyond the mere sound of their voices had a ready outlet for their letters expressing personal views. Practicing a realistic democracy, most southern editors opened their columns for a full expression of views on public issues. With a great sense of responsibility and self-importance, subscribers addressed thousands of laboriously planned and illegibly written letters to the editor, or they rushed headlong into virulent disputes with acid contempt for those who opposed their views. Whichever side the letter writers espoused mattered little in establishing the fact that the country journals were significant local sounding boards.

Even beyond the public function performed by the papers in their discussions of issues were their countless minor social services. If a subscriber's daughter ran away from home and married a notorious, drunken old rake, forty years her senior, some editors were quick to make a capital story of the blunder. Sometimes it was purely a matter of speculation as to which bride got the longer and more exciting notice, the adventurous one who clambered down a ladder and ran off to a far-distant town to begin her married life with an undesirable husband, or the one who trod primly to the altar on the arm of a willing father. At any rate neither knew beforehand whether her wedding notice would be sandwiched between advertisements of Lydia E. Pinkham's famous Vegetable Compound and of W. L. Douglas' $3.00 shoes, or interspersed with accounts of a livestock sale and of a revival meeting.

·A notice of almost every white birth in the community found its way into the local columns, and announcements of casual illnesses and all deaths were recorded there. If a first-born Southerner ever had any doubt about his legitimacy he could probably satisfy his curiosity by searching the files of his home-county paper for both the time and conditions of his parents' marriage and for a statement of his own birth. It is a joyful experience indeed to read that you were either a bouncing eight-pound boy or a precious blue-eyed girl, and to discover that your father was strutting around like he had just uncovered one of the mysterious wellsprings of nature.

Sitting at his disordered desk, the country editor received badly scribbled notes on paper sacks, pieces of wrapping paper, perfumed social stationery, and every other kind of nondescript writing material on which there was enough blank space to write out the local news. These reports came to him from many and varied sources. There were the vigilant maidens who wrote under the coquettish pen names of "Blue Eyes," "Roxana," "Dad's Pet," "Little Mary," and "Brown Hair" and who reported on all the happenings in their vicinity. Doubtless these maidens got a vicarious enjoyment out of the news of courtings and flirtations, and out of gossiping generally. With the news which came in from local reporters was that gathered by the editors from the gossips who stood about their stoves, or lolled about their doorways. This passing throng of visitors was a great source for both news and personal opinions, which were passed out with a lavish hand. Seldom was the task of news gathering a major undertaking in the business of operating a paper. Most of the time, news flowed in to the editor in a reasonable quantity. The editor's gravest responsibility was that of determining what to publish, and of evaluating the truth of the stories. In provincial rural southern communities it was not always safe to accept as statements of fact bits of news passed on by word of mouth. Always there was grave danger that the news was manufactured and colored in such a way as to embarrass one side of a community feud, and an unwary editor who published it might find himself in the midst of a fight. This danger of false news necessitated a wide personal acquaintance on the part of an editor so that he could evaluate with relative certainty not only the probability of news which came to him, but likewise the reliability of the sources from whence it came.

Not only did the common man have an opportunity to find his name in the paper because he was getting married or because he had a six-pound daughter at his house, but it got into print for many other reasons. His mules might run away, the lightning might strike his cow, his hen might lay an egg which looked like a baseball, or he might even get drunk and find his way to the "lockup." Of outstanding importance was the fact that the postwar southern papers opened a channel by which the common man could acquire the dignity of seeing his name in the paper at intervals. This ensured him a place in posterity and lifted him up to a level of esteem with his neighbors.

Southern editors worked upon the sound theory of local journalism that the way to make a living was to sell subscriptions, and that the good will of many subscribers was a highly desirable asset. One of the surest ways to cultivate good will was to follow the old country-paper maxim of "names make news."

There were the crossroads scribes who lived in little store and church communities, and who were eager to follow, in a limited way, a journalistic career. These local reporters were glad to send in their news reports in order to bring publicity to their home neighborhoods, and thereby bask in the reflected glory. Others were glad to send in collections of simple little news items once a week because they took great pride in authorship and because the honor of being a reporter gave them a feeling of superiority over the mere mortals who, in their clumsy way, were only making the news.

Everything was news. Local reporters always commented upon the weather and how it was affecting the work of the farmers, conditions of the roads, community parties, weddings, and particularly upon the progress of every courting case that showed even the remotest signs of becoming serious. Love in the rural South was a vibrant thing at all times, and much more so in the eyes of the local reporters if there was, to say the least, a slight illicit aspect to it. The local reporters were forever spilling some gallant swain's secrets to the public. They loved nothing better than to report the amorous activities of a young blade in one community, knowing very well that he was carrying on the same way in another, and that any publicity of the fact would get him into trouble with both of his love interests. Too, the reporters were not above doing a little private flirting in their own behalf, and the editor had to be alert to this fact or pretty soon he would be running several columns of nauseating flirtations for his lovelorn correspondents.

Illness, death, and religious revivals ran the weather and love a close second as matters of news interest. Being literal-minded, both local reporters and readers wanted to know in detail what happened, and the editor felt obligated to satisfy their curiosity. It was not enough to say that a neighbor was sick; it was necessary to explain what his affliction was, how much he was suffering, how well he was sleeping, what was being done for him, who his doctor was, and to speculate upon whether he would get well. The less chance for recovery the individual had, the more interesting was the report of his illness, and many an editor was forced to warn his reporters to stop writing that it was believed that there was little chance for a sick man's recovery. This might have made exciting reading for the curious subscribers, but it was rough on the morale of the patient and his family to read that the country newspaper had given up hope for him. By the same token it was not enough to say that a person had died. The full story of the manner of his dying had to be told; his last words, his expressed hope for the world beyond, and, frequently, the ghastly details of a rural funeral were printed. Religious meetings and revivals were covered with varying amounts of detail, all depending upon the emotional balance of the reporter. At least it was possible for the most unemotional reporter to give the statistical results of a warm revival in terms of conversions, sizes of crowds, and of the baptizing which followed many of them.

Characteristic of the editorial demand all over the South for local news was the request of the master of the Eufaula (Alabama) *Times and News* who begged his local correspondents not to "forget when anybody dies, gets married, runs away, steals anything, builds a house, makes a big sale, breaks his leg, or gets the senses kicked out of him by a mule, or does anything that is in anyway remarkable, and you have reason to believe you know as much about the occurrence as anybody else don't wait for someone else to report it, or trust us to find out by instinct, but come and tell us about it, or send the fact on a postal card. See if you cannot improve this year, and let us have every item of news that transpires in your neighborhood." Such invitations resulted in thousands of columns being written weekly for southern papers by young and flippant girls, solemn preachers, dignified schoolmasters, devilish old bachelors, and crotchety citizens who viewed the world through dark glasses, and who loved to editorialize on things in general. Few community secrets were kept from the prying eyes of the public. One of the very interesting studies in human psychology is to be found in the general reaction of readers to the local reports. Doubtless these features were read with more interest than any other parts of the paper, but readers generally tended to belittle the community reports with scoffing remarks. Sometimes this attitude stemmed from jealousy and animosity on the part of the reader, but the significant fact for the editor remained that the subscribers read them and asked for more.

There is almost no end to the stories of a purely personal and local nature which were printed in the southern country papers. Somewhat unconsciously editors were contemporary historians serving faithfully the ends of posterity. Week by week they compiled from their old-fashioned pyramidal California type cases a running story of provincial American life. They forged a chain description of the immediate present for the far-distant future. Through the magic door of their yellowing pages these editors made it possible to reveal the past in perhaps its most adequate form to a quizzical constituency of remote generations to come.

Concisely the southern rural paper has lived up, historically at least, to Bill Nye's declaration that it is an encyclopedia, a timetable, a poem, a history, a guide to politics, and a grand plan to a newly civilized world. A low-priced *multum in parvo,* it is a sermon, a song, a circus, an obituary, a shipwreck, a symphony in solid measure, a medley of man's glory and his shame. "It is, in short, a bird's-eye view of all the magnanimity and meanness, the joys and sorrows, the births and deaths, the pride and poverty of the world, all for a few cents."

There were, of course, local newspapers in every part of the antebellum South. Almost as soon as the settlement of a community was under way a newspaper was established, and readers had made available to them foreign, national, and political news. The antebellum papers were seldom purely local in character and almost never folksy in the flavor sense of the postwar papers. In nearly every instance the earlier papers were political vehicles which were devoted to long and vigorous essays and highly editorialized news stories supporting the editors' avowed partisan views. There were few rich local happenings recorded by the hopelessly untrained crossroads reporters, and seldom did the local wits have an opportunity to show themselves off in print. There were a few spasmodic discussions of local issues such as public roads, public schools, public health, the desirability of industry, and better personal and moral habits.

Advertisements and price currents comprise for the historian some of the most valid local sources of information to be found in the antebellum paper. Missing most of the time are the commonplace reports of the first cotton blooms, the first bale of cotton ginned, the killing of a "whopping" big snake which had crawled into the cradle with a baby, the birth of a five-legged pig, a radish with two tap roots which gave it a human-like appearance, the biggest turnip of the season, or an ear of corn with two cobs. In fact, very few stories in the earlier papers stooped to the earthy level of one appearing in the Jackson (Tennessee) *Weekly Whig and Tribune* in 1874 which told in high glee of a neighboring countryman who came into the Jackson Savings Bank with a yellow stump-tail cur at his heels to transact a minor piece of business. When he had finished at the cashier's window he left the dog behind in the bank, shut in by a newfangled glass door. "Old Yellow" became disturbed and sent up such an ungodly howl that the gentlemanly clerks were highly incensed that a stump-tail country dog was desecrating the silence of so august an institution as a bank. Armed with a broom and a long stick the clerks proceeded to give the cur the scare of his life whereupon he leaped blithely through the glass door and left his assailants behind to pay for the damage.

Although there were humorists in the Old South, not many dignified and politically-minded editors of the antebellum period would have wasted a quarter of a column of white paper and spent a precious hour, as did the master of the McDuffie (Georgia) *Journal,* setting up a rollicking piece of tomfoolery about a local hero named Squire Scroggins of Branchville, Georgia. The Squire was described as a highly excited man on this particular occasion. Nurses and doctors were dashing in and out at his place, and the Squire was seen taking lengthy swigs at a bottle containing "strengthening powders" when he was not marching around with a fence rail on his shoulders shouting, "I am the best blacksmith that ever fluttered. Could ride a bull, shoe a hyena, and hold an elephant to have his tooth pulled, and while in [my] powerful grip the average jackass is a mere toy." The editor said Squire Scroggins was cross-eyed and cross-legged, all because he had just sired a sixteen-and-a-half-pound daughter named Moriah Melody Jane Anne Scroggins.

Bill Nye's description of the American country newspaper is generally an accurate one for the local southern papers following the Civil War. Like so many southern institutions which were to play such a vital role in the postwar South, the country weekly underwent some fundamental changes in both make-up and function. Just as the mercantile business, the public school, and the state and local government became more nearly synchronized with the lives of the rural people whom they served, so did the country press.

Politically the southern papers were predominantly Democratic. It is impossible to read a postwar country paper without getting the impression that it was, as a matter of course, Democratic in politics, just as the editor was a believer in the Christian religion. Hopeful editors organized papers and saluted their prospective readers with a pledge similar to that given by the editor of the newly founded

[18]

Dickson County (Tennessee) *Press* in which he said, "We expect to be strictly Democratic and to hold up the banner of our forefathers, who one and all were strictly true to Jeffersonian Democracy—we do not believe in any third party and will endeavor to discourage the same to the best of our ability, not only because it is not Democracy but because we think it injurious to the people as a class." Perhaps political attitudes were the only distinct tie between the antebellum and postwar country weeklies. The old tone of political writing prevailed after the war. Those first meager one-page sheets which appeared with their slender advertising columns and even slenderer news columns in 1865 to 1868 were highly political in flavor. With their frail hands they fought against the Yankee influence in such matters as presidential policies, the provisional governors, the Civil Rights Bill, the three major reconstruction amendments, the numerous Congressional acts and junkets, the justification on the part of the North for establishing military governments, the fight between President Johnson and the Radicals, the effect of keeping southern political leadership at bay, the Negro in politics, and general southern resistance to northern interference in the South. Generally the news stories of these earlier years centered around Congress and the personalities of Washington. The editors were able to point up their news more clearly by translating the troubles of the Reconstruction South into terms of personalities. The growing intensity of feeling can best be savored through the weekly papers, as the Radicals began to put into practice their ill-conceived plans of readjustment. What had originally been a relatively mild southern press became highly embittered. It is a remarkable fact that the weeklies, despite their disjointed means of communication, were able to keep fairly abreast of the constantly changing picture in Washington, and this was to affect the thinking of the secession states.

Through the columns of the local papers the modern historian can trace with more than fair accuracy the metamorphosis of.the southern Democratic party. There is a picture of the party's being born locally. No other source of contemporary information offers a better human understanding of the process by which the southern party was developed. Ideologically at least, the southern-weekly editors could express in a single voice with the Meridian (Mississippi) *Mercury* that the press "should be the masters, not the bootlicks of politicians. Let newspapers boldly cry aloud and spare not, and turn the whore of Expediency out of doors. Let us have no fornicating with the Radical Party, under the idea of begetting a 'new South,' but let us nail our colors to the mast, and stand by them like men. Nothing else will save us."

Perhaps no better summary of the political temper of the southern editor can be found than the report of a survey made by the New York *Times* in 1882.

One hundred country editors in Alabama, Tennessee, Arkansas, Florida, Georgia, North Carolina, South Carolina, Louisiana, Texas, and Mississippi were asked the three questions: "(1) Is the general policy of Democratic managers in harmony with the general sentiment of people in your district? (2) How do your people regard President Arthur? (3) Is there in your neighborhood a decided expression of opinion in regard to the tariff? If so what is its extent and nature?" In summarizing its findings the *Times* concluded that the South was certainly Democratic because the southern editors believed the party would advance the region's best material and political interests. There was an expression of dissatisfaction with methods used by individual southern leaders, and their influence over local issues. For instance, there was a division in opinion in North Carolina over the stock law, but the editors everywhere were emphatic in pointing out that these differences were purely local in nature. They opposed Republicanism, and did not want the Negro to enjoy a position of political influence. As to the South's attitude toward Arthur, the people had hoped for much from Garfield, but felt that his successor was more narrowly partisan and that little good for the region could come from him. An exception to this point of view was expressed by the publishers in the three river states of Mississippi, Louisiana, and Arkansas where it was hoped some major levee work would be done. Generally the editors questioned believed their agrarian subscribers had little actual interest in the tariff. If there was an interest in the subject it was only in a tariff for revenue purposes.

On one political principle nearly all the southern weeklies were in agreement, and that was a national Democratic victory. Every paper possessed cuts of cannon booming away, full-blown flags, and numerous poses of strutting game cocks, in anticipation of the day when they could be spread on the front pages in wild acclamation of victory. These were the symbols of victory, and their appearance in a paper after general elections was a sign of unbridled celebration. After the presidential election of 1884, the editors had their first joyful opportunity to use every cut in their cases to celebrate the national victory. Along with the Marietta (Georgia) *Journal* all Democratic papers could shout hysterically: "Glorious! Solid Georgia! Boys Still Holding up the Party! The Mountain Colt refuses to be weaned! Bring out the Big Gun! Boom! Boom! A sweeping Democratic victory in New York, South Carolina, and the other States."

Since 1868 the little weeklies had hoped for just such a moment. Some of them may have been divided on local issues, and editors may have abused each other roundly because of honest differences of opinion, but they were universally jubilant over the election of Grover Cleveland. There is no way of knowing how many thousands of lines were used in the next four years in praising Cleveland, in publicizing his administration, and, occasionally, in lambasting him for what the editors considered his failure to hold high the southern standard of Democracy.

There was scarcely a moment since the Civil War when politics was not a vital issue in every weekly in the South. Every four years there were presidential campaigns, with the constant flow of Washington news stories and editorials reporting their progress. Staggered with these were the intermittent Congressional, state, and local elections which, in some states, kept in progress an almost continuous political campaign. Local elections were always good for abundant copy. Editors were more often than not forced into campaigns as supporters of one local slate or another because of the juicy plum of public printing which was at stake. In most southern counties the income from this source alone was almost enough to support a paper, and this made guessing right and winning elections vital to the economic welfare of the publishers. Not only did editors have selfish economic interest in the outcome of elections, but frequently they were candidates for office themselves. When no elections were in process, it was always possible for the papers to generate a political interest by reviewing either patronizingly or critically the acts of public officials, depending upon the interest and courage of the editors.

Fundamentally there appeared in the columns of local papers more eloquent and practical explanations of political and social attitudes than can be found in many of the more mature texts of the science of government and society. Since the moment the last gun was fired in the Civil War the whole philosophy of white supremacy has been nurtured within these columns. Apparently most editors were relatively free during the Reconstruction period to voice an expression of their philosophy upon the major issues of the moment. If they were not free in certain areas where feeling against the broader Radical principles, plus carpetbagger and scalawag activities, was most intense, there were always obliging neighbors near by who could speak out and say what they pleased. Perhaps no editor did much to check biracial and sectional hatred; some did much to plant the idea that there would come a day when Negro participation in southern politics would end. In 1890 the editor of the Greensboro (Georgia) *Herald* reviewed the last seven years of Georgia politics in which the Negro had held a possible balance of power in the state, and concluded that racial and social strife had increased and that Negroes were debauched by believing lies told them against the white man and by the use of whisky at the polls. Negro crimes against white women were said to be increasing, and friction between the two races was growing rapidly. The *Herald* was dedicated to solidifying the white vote, and asked

[24]

that no man be elected to office except by a white primary. Nine years later this paper had the same convictions. "Everybody," said the editor, "must be elected by a white primary." Scrambling for Negro votes degraded the white man, thought the Barnesville (Georgia) *Gazette*. Deluded and immoral Negro voters were the greatest curse of the age and could best be relegated to sections which laid no claim to enlightenment. These were the sentiments of a long list of exchanges.

By 1900 the white-supremacy pattern was well developed. Elimination of Negro suffrage from the political scene by constitutional restriction in most of the southern states was looked upon by the country press as a monumental advance in regional good government and white dignity. This was the final process of sweeping away the last evidence of hated Reconstruction, and, incidentally, of the threat of third partyism. Only one serious political ogre stood in the way, and that was the fear that some attempt might be made by a Republican President and Congress to use the Fourteenth Amendment to reduce southern representation in Congress. A majority of the southern editors could close their journalistic careers after new constitutions were adopted with sentiments similar to those expressed by John S. Reynolds in his valedictory upon retirement from the editorship of the Winnsboro (South Carolina) *News and Herald*. He wrote: "I have sought to be guided by but one consideration—the good of the people (I mean the white people) of South Carolina. . . . I have been, at times, the subject of covert criticism more severe than just— this because I have chosen, after my own fashion, to protest against certain things calculated to make a breach in the Party."

Closer home, and safely out of reach of the tentacles of the Republican party, southern editors had mixed political emotions. They could at times be caustic in their criticism of home-grown politicians. Sitting well back away from the confusing maelstrom of state-capital politics, they were able to analyze the devious processes of government in most unflattering terms to the actors on the stage. At Stanford, Kentucky, the forthright Virginia Democrat W. P. Walton, of the *Interior Journal,* believed "The average legislator is a fraud, a delusion and a snare. Kentucky's late conglomeration of imbecility passes a school law which a Philadelphia lawyer couldn't for the life of him tell whether it calls for three or two cents, and now we hear that Tennessee's menagerie of incompetents failed in reapportioning the state to mention three of its counties at all, which it is said may, if not corrected, vitiate every congressman elected under it."

Closely akin to Colonel Walton's opinion of the Kentucky and Tennessee legislators was that expressed by the editor of the Choctaw (Alabama) *Herald* who said the "Montgomery Menagerie closed its exhibition on last Tuesday night at 12. A large number of them can bid safely adieu to the capitol city as they will never have an occasion to visit it again, at least at the expense of the state." There was the same general feeling expressed toward both Congressmen and state representatives as was found in the much-publicized prayer of the great preacher T. DeWitt Talmadge which was uttered at the end of a service in the New York Academy of Music. He prayed: "We thank Thee that the congress of the nation has departed, and that many of those who represented the people in public offices will no more represent them. We pray that You will forgive them for the damage they have done the nation."

It was necessary for the weekly papers to rein up short the politicians for their indifference to public needs, their stupid mistakes, and, sometimes, for their overzealousness. So long as an official was a Democratic product of a white primary he was public property to most of the local editors. He had to be as tough as W. P. Ford's mule which fell into a deep clay pit in northern Georgia and almost starved to death before he was discovered. Just as soon as the mule was released he made for feed and water. He would have perished under the mistreatment and starvation, said his owner, had it not been for the fact that he was a Democrat and was waiting around to hear the joyous tidings of victory in the mid-term elections of 1882. Actually the country papers were frequently unenthusiastic over the products of their local Democratic primaries as a means for strengthening the powers of representative government. From the editorial point of view the average southern state during the meeting of its legislature was often like a punch-drunk fighter staggering around the ring waiting frantically for the gong to sound and save it from a knockout.

Every four years in some states and every two in others the gubernatorial race made capital news. Seldom did an editor remain neutral. At an early stage in the campaign, the local paper got into the fight as a hot partisan in favor of one of the candidates. For instance, in Mississippi, editors lined up during the first two decades of the present century as either Vardaman or anti-Vardaman partisans, and they printed full column after column of their fellow editor's sulphurous outpourings either to praise or to scorn him. Hundreds of special news stories were published, and this famous demagogue's every move was followed by wide publicity. In South Carolina, "Pitchfork" Ben Tillman enjoyed the same distinction, and so did Bob and Alf Taylor in Tennessee, Kolb, Oates, Jelks, and Heflin in Alabama, and a long string of politicians in Georgia from Joe Brown to Eugene Talmadge. Certainly no politician in the South could hope for political success without a modicum of country-press support.

Political campaigns were not always fought out

among the rival editors on the grounds of basic issues and personalities involved. Often the papers became embroiled with each other in petty personal editorial jealousies and disputes which were every bit as bitter as those of the candidates. Occasionally the exchange of editorial fire was rapid and hot. One publisher often took another to task and called for specific answers to embarrassing questions. If it happened that there were two papers in the same town a bitter rivalry was sure to occur. Usually the average southern town offered too little advertising to support even a single paper, and if a rival appeared it became necessary to get rid of it by one means or another. The best time to do this was during a warm political campaign when there was a chance that a competitor could be forced into a position where he would have to express an opinion which would do him irreparable harm with his subscribers. So intense and personal has politics been in the South that it was not unusual for editors to use their fists on each other, and a few have been known to challenge their competitors to a more permanent and business-like way of settling their arguments. Just as often, there have been great storms of noise and editorial jabbing going on which in the end proved to be nothing more than a subtle device for keeping reader interest at a high level. The editor who could trap an opponent in statements which could be interpreted as reflecting upon the white primary or derogatory to white supremacy could

[29]

virtually wipe him out of business. There was little sense of ethics among the earlier postwar southern editors to cause them to keep their professional rivalries undercover as did the physicians and lawyers. They brought their issues out in the public print for all to see.

Just as the editors jousted with each other, so they did with subscribers. A free press allowed editors to determine their own political and social views and to establish certain personal loyalties. But freedom from a legalistic point of view was one thing, and from a practical point an altogether different one. Readers frequently became incensed at what they read in the paper, and bombarded the editor with letters of personal abuse in order to warn that the embittered masses considered they had an inalienable vested interest in the paper and its political views without being involved financially beyond the price of a year's subscription. This fact led occasionally to considerable friction and many attempts to embroil editors in open fist fights. One north Mississippi editor was said to have had three fights on the day the first issue of his paper appeared. Whipping the editor was often more than a joke with irate patrons, and not until the age of twentieth-century gentility was well advanced was this fascinating pastime discontinued.

It is safe to say that success or failure in politics in the South can be accurately gauged over a period of years by the general leaning of the editors and their papers. No one can measure the absolute effect of the local press in a given election, but over a long period of time the influence no doubt has been tremendous. It is hardly necessary to quibble over the issue of whether the paper influenced popular reaction to the basic southern issues, or whether it climbed on the band wagon and followed along in the wake of a militantly aroused public opinion. In nearly every county there was an editor who was a self-appointed preserver of his reading public's sacred political and social mores and prejudices, and during every election or social upheaval he brought them out and kept them on public display for all to view and take heed. Editors who enjoyed the most success were generally those whose constant dealing with the printed word gave them, in the eyes of their readers, a sacrosanct wisdom far above that possessed by their fellow men, and consequently it was not too difficult for them to sway major segments of public opinion in every election or community campaign. In fact the editor's chair was not an altogether undesirable place from which to launch a successful political campaign. Many famous names in southern politics were also prominent among the editorial fraternity. Of these it is only necessary to mention James K. Vardaman, Tom Watson, W. D. Jelks, Bob Taylor, and Urey Woodson. Scores of country editors found it relatively easy to get into county offices, and often they went to state capitals as legislators. Some of them even went to Congress or to highly desirable appointive jobs within the power of gift by party chieftains.

Just as the weekly papers reflected the political flavor of the postwar South, so did they mirror faithfully and tangibly the cultural level of the region. In two significant areas, especially, there are few better sources for gauging accurately the true conditions of the various phases of social development for the past seventy-five years. County journalists early acknowledged with a blunt frankness the lack of education on the part of their people. They were quick to realize the correlation of their patrons' ability to read and what constituted news for them. Many of their editorials, special-feature articles, and news stories were written in a friendly vein, couched in the simple semi-illiterate vernacular of the backwoods community, and highly flavored with dashes of folk humor. Characteristic of this method of writing for the country reader were the enormously popular columns written from almost the end of the Civil War through the Theodore Roosevelt period by Bill Arp of Georgia. Arp's columns were dialectic, humorous, opinionated, and extremely influential. He was a master at interpreting the prejudices of readers all over the South, and of expressing them with exactness in the language of the semi-illiterate so as to mold the reader's thinking into a definitely limited provincial thought pattern which precluded any other explanation of an issue. No one has yet discovered this important personal influence in a modern study of the southern mind and properly appraised its author in an analysis of the shaping of southern public opinion. To understand the philosophy and methodology of Bill Arp is to grasp a fundamental knowledge of the intellectual development of much of the New South.

The average southern editor might bemoan the lack of educational advantages in his community in one column and cater directly to a semifrontier pride in lack of education in another. Often editors in discussing the important subject of educational needs were in the situation of a man who writes on a blackboard with one hand and busily erases what he has written with the other. Always, however, there was indication of an oblique awareness and acknowledgment of the South's backwardness in keeping abreast of the rising tide of progressiveness elsewhere in the country. So long as this criticism was allowed to arise and be expressed in a southern community the needs were made known in the press. But most editors were extremely intolerant of criticisms which came from the outside, and especially of those which originated on the wrong side of the Potomac. The moment a Northerner became critical of the South's lack of social and cultural advantages he faced a stone wall in the curt observation of the southern local press that conditions were equally as bad if not worse in other sections of the country.

Since 1865 local southern publishers have adopted the notion that the daily papers published in the larger centers had the edge on them in reporting national and foreign news. They had national and foreign news services as well as telegraph and reportorial facilities for distributing such highly current matter. The true function of the country paper was to editorialize the national and foreign intelligence and to print only local news, or special "evergreen" features which appealed to local reader interest. This tended to nurture local southern provincialism, which over the years crystallized into a state of mind in which, in many communities, any new idea requiring a change of thought and habit was greeted with hostility.

During the first four decades after the war many rural areas of the New South failed to develop an educational system adequate enough to enable large numbers of people to read the simple news stories which were printed in the country papers. In 1902 it was said by the Ellisville (Mississippi) *News* that Mississippi was one of the poorest newspaper states in the Union; only sparsely settled Arizona and Nevada ranked lower. There were only seven papers in the state which exceeded a thousand circulation. It was generally true, however, that the average country paper in Mississippi wielded more influence within its community per copy distributed than anywhere else because there was less competition from the outside daily papers and periodicals. But editors could take little satisfaction in this fact because of the staggering and inert barrier of illiteracy athwart their paths. The editor of the *News* reflected with wisdom that considerable headway had to be made in "reducing illiteracy, ignorance, and lack of public spirit" before the newspaper could prosper. Mississippi was not alone in its educational problems. Elsewhere in the South newspapers were seriously handicapped because of large numbers of illiterate people in their counties. These people not only did not subscribe to the papers, but they were unable to take editorial advice and work toward an improvement of community conditions. So acutely aware was the Kentucky legislature of this general cultural condition that a bill was introduced in that body proposing that a country paper be sent at state expense to every family. It was argued that this was the most effective way to reduce illiteracy in every age group in the state.

Just as educational levels determined to a great extent the fortune of local papers, so did the economic level of the communities. Country editors could hope to survive only by acquiring a certain number of paid-up subscribers. They, of course, took great satisfaction from the fact that their papers' editorial influence was impressive; but after all, their animal needs were food, shelter, and clothing. Some editors were threatened constantly with failure because of lack of patronage. The circulation of no southern weekly was ever fabulous. It usually averaged five to eight hundred, and when patrons refused to pay their subscription bills the editors were left in a sad financial plight. Reminders appeared in papers begging subscribers to pay up, if not in money, then in edible produce. Often publishers would specify at certain seasons of the year what produce they deemed most acceptable on subscription bills. In 1893 it was said that a Tennessee publisher was to speak before the Chicago meeting of the National Editorial Association on the subject: "The Country Editor in Clover, or, How to Get Fat on Cordwood and Promises." One jocular scribe wrote of his ill-fated financial venture in the field of country journalism: "It is with a feeling of sadness that we retire from the control of this paper, but we leave our journal with a gentleman who is abler, financially, to handle it. This gentleman is well known in this county. He is the sheriff." E. H. Aull of the Newberry (South Carolina) *Herald and News* wrote in 1890 of the woes of an editor, saying that the delinquent subscriber was a chronic problem, as were the unpaid advertising accounts, but the biggest concern of an editor was that of filling a paper with respectable news. The tariff was too technical, and besides it was a threadbare subject which had been discussed so much in the papers that it even smelled of printer's ink. Nearly every editor in South Carolina had voiced an acid opinion at one time or another of the Farmers' Alliance, and the farmers had been freely advised on the complex problems of raising more food and less cotton, and upon the impending industrialization of the South. Yet with all these problems the editor was able to make his readers believe that he actually enjoyed living.

When the editor of a southern country paper grew despondent and began to brood over his earthly plight, a ubiquitous exchange would always bring to mind the ancient story, which had appeared at one time or another in nearly every paper published, of the country newspaperman who stood before the main gate of hell and sought admission on the merits of his editorial past. But the devil refused to grant his request on the grounds that, "For years thou hast borne the blame of errors that printers made in the papers. The paper has gone, alas, for $2 and the $2 have often failed to come in. The printers have bedeviled thee for wages Saturday nights. Thou hast been called a dead beat by the passenger conductors when thou hast shown thy annual pass to their envious gaze—all these things thou didst. Thou canst come in here." As the gate was closed in his face, the editor heard the devil remark to one of his minions, "Heaven is his home, and besides if we had let him in here he would have been continually dunning his delinquent subscribers, and thus create discord in my kingdom."

Most editors, despite their constant financial worries, were not wholly unappreciative of their positions of honor in their communities. They realized that a well-conducted paper was a distinct asset to their counties, and where they were able to disturb the public mind and break up local inertia they could take great pride in things accomplished. Very few, however, could boast of success, as did that Arkansas editor who said he had become a publisher in order to get elected to office, and he had succeeded and was retiring to give another man a chance. In his valedictory he wrote, "I have made many friends and killed two men during my editorial career for which I am thankful and deeply indebted to this community."

II

NEWS FOR THE PEOPLE

Fantastic stories made news for country readers. Few subscribers became worried either about the
propriety or basic truth of impersonal accounts
which they read in local papers. Apparently the more
unreasonable a story was the more readable it became. A wild yarn set afloat among the newspaper
exchanges in 1887 by the Pascagoula *Democrat-Star*
explained that a group of enterprising Alabama capitalists proposed to raise black tomcats for the
European mink market. Their scheme, once started,
was to be a type of perpetual motion among the black
cats. The choice animals were to be fed on the carcasses of the undesirable greys and spots. Once a crop
of the ebony-hued ones had been matured, their flesh
was to be fed back to the younger ones. An expert
figured out a ratio of probability, and he believed that
100,000 blacks would produce 25,000 greys, and a
return of $1,200,000 was a reasonable expectation of
income. The company wanted to buy 5,000 black tomcats, and 100,000 black females—the entire batch

to be paid for in Sheffield Landing building lots.

This was one of the methods which editors in sleepy southern hamlets and towns employed to keep their columns filled. The black-tomcat story was a good exchange-paper joke which went the rounds. Editors grew weary searching for news stories that were serious and reasonable, and they finally gave in and published every bit of nonsense which came to hand.

Despite the use of stories like the one about mink skins from black cats, editing a country newspaper was, to all intents and purposes, a serious business. Editors, however, like a majority of their readers, had a keen relish for human-interest stories. Not only did the average publisher make his paper a political and social conscience for his subscribers, but he also made it a source of amusement and relaxation. Often special-feature stories which filled one or more columns were so placed that they immediately caught the eye of the casual reader. There were brief items of two to ten lines which were primarily space fillers, and news items only by the most liberal interpretation. In this particular field of journalism the average post–Civil War southern mind stands revealed. The Southerner was fond of the unusual, the jocular, and most of all the everyday wisdom expressed in a continuous stream of editorial observations. This type of editorializing had to be brief, as did almost every other story which was printed. It was necessary to catch the reader's attention, and at the same time to reduce the labor of setting type and to conserve meager space. Of fundamental importance was the apparent realization that the average subscriber could absorb with ease only short snatches of news.

Country readers liked sensational stories. The misadventures of nature were the best sources of news for the average country editor. Bored with a solitary existence, the rural patron welcomed accounts of the unusual. Living close to the soil, the countryman had a ready appreciation of freaks of nature which made periodic appearances. Mother Nature occasionally seemed to forget her dignity to perform some amusing capers, and these never ceased to be newsworthy.

One of the easiest ways for a constituent to get his name into the news, aside from getting married or shooting someone, was to discover and deliver to a newspaper office a freak of nature. As a result of this particular kind of news interest the average print shop often took on the atmosphere of a museum for the display of the abnormalities of nature. There were tall stalks of corn, heavily laden cotton plants, bundles of oats, large potatoes, unusual eggs, and, sometimes, for brief periods, the carcasses of deformed animals, strange bugs, long, sinuous snakes, roots of trees which gave the appearance of everything from a cross to the Hunchback of Notre Dame, old-fashioned tools, guns, and pieces of weird local whittling. Editors were many times bedeviled by publicity-seeking nuisances who brought in these unusual

things and demanded "puffs." In fact, it was prob-
lematical as to which could consume the most time
and ask for the most space, publicity-seeking subscribers with strange objects to display or local poets
whose tender souls overflowed with every change of
the weather.

Much of the human-interest news in the country
paper had a common origin with the regional folklore.
Near Wickliffe, Kentucky, an argument raged over
the ancient question as to whether persimmon trees
grew from the bodies of grubworms. C. C. Terrill
was certain they did and brought to the editor of the
Ballard (Kentucky) *News* a worm with a persimmon
sprout growing from its mouth. It mattered little to
the editor that Terrill had failed to distinguish between the germ of the persimmon seed, which looks
exactly like a worm, and an honest-to-goodness grub-
worm. To him this was a story worthy of a paragraph,
and it would not displease his subscribers, for most of
them were already convinced that persimmon trees
were produced in this unorthodox manner. Not only
were such bits of local superstition well received by
the home people, but they were honored elsewhere by
editors who used them in their exchange columns.
This latter fact demonstrated to the original publisher
that he was held in some esteem by his confreres when
they were willing to excerpt his material.

When a farmer discovered the slightest hint that
nature was a bit "out of kilter" he rushed in to report

the fact as though it were a world-shaking matter. A peach tree which bore peaches on one branch and plums on another was a curiosity, and when such a phenomenon occurred the editor was informed at once. The strange branches were sawed off and taken into town to wilt and die in the newspaper-office window. Often a subscriber bought a batch of fruit trees from an itinerant agent and was utterly amazed that they bore fruit which only remotely resembled that displayed in the beautifully lithographed catalogue, and he took into town a generous sample of fruit for the editor. A patron deposited a box of fruit on the printer's desk and then drove home to await the coming of the paper on Saturday morning to see what the editor had to say about it.

One type of seasonal news which appeared in southern papers was strictly characteristic of the South. Each year three stories were printed in the papers with the regularity of the changing seasons. When a farmer found the first square on a cotton plant and the first bloom, he felt morally bound to crow about it in the local paper. Editors had to be quick-witted to determine whether a patron had actually found a cotton blossom or whether he was palming off an althea bloom. In late summer and early fall issues of every paper in the cotton belt there appeared notices of the first bales of cotton ginned. "Greensboro received her first bale of cotton on Thursday, August 20," wrote the editor of the Greensboro

(Georgia) *Herald.* "Young Davis, colored, brought it in. It sold for $.12½, or a premium of $.03. This Negro brought first bale last season." No southern farmer ever took more pride in an accomplishment than he did in being the first one to find a cotton bloom or to gin the first bale of cotton. In the first instance there was little more reward than the mere catering to one's vanity. For the producer of the first bale of cotton ginned there was a premium price as well as a more lengthy notice in the paper.

Reporting things extraordinary was not always troublesome for the editor. Despite the fact that this particular aspect of local journalism brought loafers into the print shop, and "puff" seekers were legion, there was real news value in much of this material. Also, better than half of the unusual things brought in to be "puffed" about were highly edible. It was not difficult at all to find space enough to give notice to a patron's generosity in leaving an old ham at the office, or to get out the New Year's edition after having received a half-dozen glasses of rich, foamy eggnog that spoke with genuine authority of a reader's thoughtfulness of the printer. No subscriber could ask with good grace for space to report his unusually fine peaches, grapes, or delicious apples without leaving a generous sample behind. Monstrous watermelons and gallon buckets of fine, bright molasses had a way of remaining behind in the newspaper office as tokens of appreciation. In springtime, when human activity was being speeded up to meet the demands of the season, both food and news became fairly scarce. Local reporters sometimes had to give up in desperation on the grounds that farmers were very busy and there was nothing for them to write about. This made any subject which could be converted into a paragraph almost as much appreciated as the more tangible gifts which appeared in the form of fruits and vegetables.

High on the list of unusual human-interest stories which always attracted major attention were those labeled *lusus naturae*. A main source of these stories of abnormality was the chicken yard, where hens, lacking enough calcium in their diet to supply the heavy drain being made upon their systems in a busy laying season, often made startling blunders in the task of producing eggs. In fact, there seems to have been no end to the oddities which came from hens' nests. As the editor of the Hickman (Tennessee) *Pioneer Press* said, "An egg 'has been laid' on our table which is rather a curiosity. It is about the size of a common hen egg and has a snout or handle about three inches long protruding from the little end. It was laid by a hen in the jail yard." Eggs of almost every known shape, color, and size were dropped in nests within the territory of every paper published in the South. There were the famous eggs with the mysterious and imaginary letter "W" which was supposed to have signified war. These eggs were supposed to be stern prophecies that there was an immediately impending crisis. There were eggs with human faces, eggs with laced seams which resembled baseballs, and eggs that were Siamese twins with connecting calcareous tubes. In a Mississippi paper the editor ran a picture of a "baseball" egg, and gave its politically ambitious owner a write-up which seemed to indicate that it was he and not his "dominecker" hen who laid it.

A turkey gobbler in South Carolina defied all of the laws of masculine nature. He got almost as much publicity in Lewis M. Grist's famous Yorkville *Enquirer* as did the Lost Cause and the prospective candidates for the governorship combined. All the gobbler did to get written up in the paper was to sit patiently upon a nest of miniature eggs until they were hatched, and then mother the tiny fledglings until they were ready to shift for themselves. The fact that the gobbler was a good sitter and an attentive "mother" was news within itself, but what had made him a thing of wonderment was the fact that he had sat upon guinea eggs and later had been able to keep up with a nervous, scurrying brood of brown chicks. This was a subject for speculation and discussion long after the paper had turned yellow with age and the guineas had found their way into the family pot. In many instances, such stories were clipped and pasted in scrapbooks to be retained and read again in after years.

Just as hens and turkey gobblers assisted in dis-

turbing the equilibrium of nature, so did human be-
ings. A Kentucky woman gave birth to a one-pound
baby whose face could be covered with a silver dollar
and whose body could be concealed in a quart cup.
The Paris editor said, "The child is normal in every
way." In Rock Hill, South Carolina, a Negro girl
gave birth to a child who was somewhat a biological
overprint in that it had four ears, a double nose,
double eyelashes, and other abnormal features. The
Spartanburg (South Carolina) *Herald* reported a
boy born in Newberry County who had a tail several
inches long, and said that as the child grew older he
could wiggle the tail like a dog and throw doubt upon
the whole story of Genesis. It was a matter of pride
with both the boy and his family that he had a tail,
and his mother was reported to have made him three-
legged trousers, with two legs for the usual purposes
and the third for his caudal appendage. This was
indeed a *lusus naturae* which enjoyed the distinction
of being both a first-class curiosity and excellent exchange material. In Newberry County this boy was a
great curiosity, and he attracted almost as much attention as did the famous Cole Blease.

The South Carolina boy with a tail was only a minor
lapse of nature. A Tennessee woman, in 1881, was reported to have given birth to seven girl babies at one
time. Conservative editors wrote that this astounding
incident "was attracting some attention." News accounts seem to intimate that it was a strange thing

that the father was elated, even though he was a bit puzzled as to how, later on in life, he would be able to clothe so many girls at one time. In the most matter-of-fact way the editor of the local paper said, "the seven babies, while not large, weighing from four to five pounds each, appear to be healthy, well-developed children." The father was said to be a spare-made man, and his wife was strong and healthy. "A most singular feature of the children is that all of them have blue eyes, and so closely resemble each other that it is hard to tell 'which from t'other.' " Whether or not this story has the slightest basis in fact is unknown, but such a sensational happening had a genuine news value which would have permitted considerably more spectacular exploitation. Perhaps editors in the South had their sense of the unusual so badly blunted by the tricks of nature that seven girl babies in a brood was scarcely more exciting than fifteen bird pups born in a single litter.

The animal kingdom in bringing forth its young could be counted upon to do the unusual with a degree of regularity. Domesticated livestock, even though it has lived for centuries in close proximity to man, has never gotten away from some of its primitive instincts, and has mixed man-made conditions with those of nature in a comical fashion. One of these lapses was described in a sober social note written by a local correspondent for the *Allen County* (Kentucky) *News*. The reporter said that "Durward Powell, who lives near the Devashier School House, had a sow to disappear last week for a couple of days, located her in a hayloft with a litter of six pigs. The animal had climbed several steps in search of a bed and considering the severe cold which prevailed, we would say for a dumb animal that was mighty good judgment."

Always the dramatic acts of animals had a great fascination for the rural Southerner. Especially was this true if a slightly humorous turn could be given a story in which some accident had befallen an animal because of man's erratic activities. Near Pulaski, Tennessee, William Butler's milch cow wandered up to a country schoolhouse where a singing school was in progress. Being somewhat blinded by the lights in the schoolhouse and completely dumbfounded by the ungodly noise made by the singers, the beast stepped into an old-fashioned open dug well. So thunderous, in fact, was her passage down to the subterranean depths that she disrupted the singing master's immediate plans. No longer could he keep his tuneful scholars concerned with their notes and chords. To begin with, the editor of the Pulaski *Citizen* was out of sympathy with the singing school, and when it was broken up by so unmusical an animal as a blundering milch cow he had as good an excuse as he wanted to laugh it out of existence. Speculating upon the cow's motives and sad plight, he wrote: "She had been electrified by the sweet sounds, and was doubtless attempting to trip the light fantastic hoof and thus became dazed; and remembering the couplet that advises the revelers to drink deep of the pierian spring, she concluded a well would answer [the purpose] so she started down for a draught. The poet didn't recommend which end went foremost, however, and so our kine friend happened to advance backward into her fancied summer resort, and realizing her mistake before she commenced to imbibe its innocuous draught, she concluded to lodge halfway down, and lodging she stuck, and sticking she bellowed. Strange to say, the people were aroused by the bellowing, notwithstanding the singing school was in full blast, with blue streaks of melody streaming out the windows and a ravishing deluge of enchanting lava threatening to engulf the village and stifle its denizens with immoderate harmony. They rushed to her rescue and soon her exploit was a tale that was told, and also a tail that was pulled. They got her out by one horn and her dilemma and she walked off as placidly as if she had been to a funeral on a free bus, and two minutes by the town pump she had bit off the only tufts of grass within three miles of the station. Her tail hung along behind her like the drag rope of a balloon, but it pops every few moments like bones strung together."

Not even a cow lodged in a well at a singing school could surpass the snake stories. In all the history of southern country newspapers, it is safe to say, no sub-

[50]

ject was more fascinating than the bloodcurdling activities of man's original tormentors, the serpents of spring. Shrewdly, editors realized that if their papers became dull for a lack of news all they had to do was to ferret out a first-rate snake story and immediately they would quicken the flagging interest of their readers. Even those gentle patrons whose whole nature rebelled at the thought of such a repulsive thing read the stories because of their fatal attraction. Snakes even ran local politicians a close second for space in the weeklies. Just about the time the first buds of the trees were beginning to change into rabbit ears of leaf clusters, farmers were daily uncovering serpentine horrors in their fields. "Snakes are beginning to appear," wrote the editor of the Toccoa (Georgia) *News* in June, 1885. "Mr. Cobb held a big moccasin in his lap for about one, one-hundreth of a second. 'He didn't go to do it.' " Colonel R. F. Nesbitt, near Marietta, was a little more intimate in his association with His Snakeship. He went out on the Powder Springs Road to do some work and threw his coat on the ground. The next morning when he was getting ready to leave his house for preaching he ran a hand in a side pocket of the coat to see what made it so heavy and was somewhat shocked to have a snake coil itself about his arm. It was said that the Colonel "got lively" all at once. But certainly Colonel Nesbitt's coat was not so much a burden to him as was the large, flower-trimmed Victorian hat of a young lady who

[51]

lived near Rome, Georgia. She went into town shop-
ping, and after a long, tiresome day she returned
home and asked her sister to assist in removing her
hat because it was so heavy and her neck was so tired
from carrying it. The sister jumped back in surprise
when she discovered that a large snake was coiled in
the decoration just ready to strike.

Every paper had to run at least one snake-
allurement story a year to retain its position of re-
spectability in the community. In Alabama, J. A. Guyn
was walking near his home when he heard a sound
like that of a stifled katydid. On approaching the
source of the noise he saw a cat gazing intently at
something in the weeds, and not far away he discovered a large rattlesnake with uplifted head and tail,
its satanic eyes focused intently upon the cat. The
snake was making a monotonous sound and was lur-
ing the cat on to certain death. Such an account
bordered on the realm of folk mysticism, and there
is grave doubt, of course, as to its validity, but this
did not keep it from being good news copy for a
frantic editor who saw a publication deadline creep-
ing upon him. In a barren season for news, press days
sometimes had the same sinister meaning for publishers as that with which the rattler approached the cat.

Any kind of snake story was good in a land where
the misdeeds of Eve with the original serpent were as
realistic as were those of the moccasins and rattle-
snakes which made every weed-grown path across a

swampy place in the South a veritable trail of horror. If a story involved an awesome experience with a rattlesnake it was indeed one of major interest. There was Mrs. Joe McCloskey of Cumberland, Kentucky, who felt something heavy pass over her face. When she made a light she discovered it was a rattlesnake and that it was in the bed with her children. At first the mother was stiff with fright, but after a moment she recovered her nerve and with a single stroke ended the sinuous intruder's existence. A like situation was that which occurred on a coon hunt near Abbeville, South Carolina. The huntsmen were stretched out on the ground waiting for the dogs to strike a trail, when one of them heard the faint sound of a rattler dragging his rattles against the rocky surface, and warned his companions to lie perfectly still. In a moment a large snake crawled across one of the boys from head to foot, passed over another's face, and then over the bill of the cap of a third. In all, six snakes went by in precisely the same path. This destroyed the youth sportsmen's zest for night hunting, and gave the editor of the Abbeville (South Carolina) *Press and Banner* a full column of hair-raising space filler.

Some papers ran regular columns of these strange snake stories from all over the South as exchange material. To the Southerner living in a heavily wooded and swampy country nothing could be more interesting than the eerie snake tales which appeared annually in the weekly papers. They were important because they involved the sinful doings of man's most ancient deceiver. This kind of feature material was peculiar to the South and Southwest. It was the ancient and threadbare sea-serpent yarn of the seafaring coastal communities converted into a southern regional pattern, and so much of it was the common yearly experience of the country reader that it gave him exciting conversational material for weeks. Snake stories were contemporary legends in the process of becoming folk tales and tall stories. This type of copy lived longest in reader interest.

Horror stories in any form were popular. It was but a short journalistic step from those telling of narrow escapes from snakes to those relating to ghosts. In the main it was only a matter of shifting emphasis from a fear of the tangible to that of the intangible. Over and over, long, rambling accounts of spectral appearances were presented as factual reporting. There was the famous case of the screaming apparition which spent some time scaring the citizens of Fort Gaines, Alabama, into resolving to give up their joyful experiences of sinning and to beg forgiveness for all their past indiscretions. On J. B. Grimsley's farm there occurred ungodly and intermittent spasms of human screaming and moaning which caused even the most guiltless souls to hasten away panic-stricken. Hundreds of persons went to be frightened by the agonizing shouts, and fled to speculate on the source

of so unnatural a phenomenon. Bold and intelligent
men, it was said by the editor of the Eufaula (Alabama) *Times and News,* came away feeling that the
ghost of a murdered man visits the place and the
horrible wails emanate from his lost soul.

Some souls did not wait until they were irretriev-
ably lost before making copy for the country newspapers. There was an army of corpses who made
headlines by dramatically sitting up in their coffins
just before the lids were lowered for the last time and
asking calmly what was happening to them. Soon after her wedding, Mary Griffith of Baltimore fell
down some steps and injured herself, and death was
apparently the result. In a short time her body was
prepared for burial, and it lay in state two days. The
funeral service was completed, the family had taken
the last tearful look at the body, and the undertaker
was about to close the coffin when he discovered that
his victim had developed a pronounced lifelike appearance. A physician was summoned, the bride was
found to be alive, and she stepped from her coffin into
the arms of her groom and family.

Many of the hundreds of published death and
burial stories were much more morbid than the last-
minute revival of Mary Griffith. Less-alert under-
takers completed their tasks and packed their patrons
away under four or five feet of clay and left them to
the fate of the dead. If innumerable stories are to be
credited, an astounding number of people were

buried alive. Graves were opened for the purpose of moving bodies from one graveyard to another, and often it was found that the remains were turned upside down. There seems to have been a general psychosis of fear that people would be buried before they had expired. It seems to have been a popular belief that under many conditions a person in a coma would simulate death and would be buried.

Martha Smith of Chatham County, North Carolina, was somewhat more fortunate than numerous corpses whose skeletons were found in reverse positions. She owned several rings and a fine watch which she admired so much that she requested that at her death they be buried with her body. When she died her wish was granted, and news of the request concerning the jewelry was given publicity. On the second night after her burial, a Negro and a white vandal raised the coffin, and when they removed the lid their victim sat up and asked what they wanted. At that particular moment their greatest desire was a wide, open strip across the long end of Chatham County in which to do some immediate traveling. Martha Smith, however, was anxious to be off home and was needlessly afraid to go unaccompanied; so she commanded her white disturber to go with her, grave clothes and all, to her husband's door. When her knock was answered by her bereaved spouse he took one look and fainted, but soon the couple was reunited, and, in the very best Victorian tradition, they lived to ripe old ages.

The story of Martha Smith's resurrection has lived long after her time. It, along with similar yarns, became the germ of an idea for accounts of persons being buried alive. These stories were printed in full columns of close-set type, and their high degree of reader interest brought subscribers back begging for more material of a like nature. Whether or not a single corpse ever sat up in a coffin before a startled family and demanded to know what was going on, or a single one ever came back from the grave after having been buried, or whether there is some reasonable physical explanation as to why many skeletons were turned upside down is beside the point. Country-newspaper editors, readyprint publishers, and feature writers in general recorded these happenings. Much of the postwar southern mentality appears to have been morbid. The horrors of country graveyards were real ones, and it was not too difficult to develop ghostly folk legends about such matters. Aside from reflecting, somewhat, the mental attitudes of the average reader, these stories are also highly reflective of the lack of medical care and advice for the people. Death often occurred with no medical assistance present, and there was ever an uncertainty in the minds of family and friends as to the actual condition of the victim. There was a dread of being too hasty in making such a decision, and this resulted in unusually long and unpleasant wakes in which to determine the fact that death had really occurred. Perhaps modern use of embalming fluids generally served to end these stories. Likewise certain doctors made it a point to relieve the public mind of these tortures by assuring aggrieved readers that there was scant possibility that their loved ones could live in a casket long enough to turn over.

Editors shifted the spirit of their feature stories with utter abandon. It may be true that the average country journalist grew sufficiently wise in his trade to appreciate the fact that psychologically there was indeed a thin border line between certain types of intense morbidity and humor. At least they crossed this line at will, and seemed oblivious of the fact that they had shifted emotional directions. Humor of a rugged semifrontier quality was an extremely popular newspaper feature. Every piece of regional dialect and wit which could be copied sooner or later made the exchange rounds of the southern papers. One common trick was for an editor to pretend that someone had brought into his office a letter which had been dropped accidentally on a back-country road by a highly romantic but unschooled Lothario whose passion of love was considerably more developed than was his knowledge of grammar. Many of these letters were illiterate babblings which were humorous only in their conscious misspellings and incongruous use of words. A little more finished and imaginative is the following letter which was attributed to ardent lovers in almost every part of the South. "Dear Amelia," wrote this moon-struck gallant, "My love is stronger than patent butter, or the kick of a young cow, sensations of joy go through me like cohorts of ants through an army cracker, and capers [*sic*] over my heart like goats on a stable roof. I feel as though I could lift myself by my boot straps to the height of a church steeple, or like an old stage horse in a green pasture. As a mean pup hankers after sweet milk, so do I hanker after your presence. And as the goslin swimeth in the mud puddle, so do I swim in a sea of delightfulness when you are near me. My heart flaps up and down like a churn dasher, and my eyes stand open like cellar doors in a country town, and if my love is not reciprocated I will pine away and die, like a poisoned bedbug and you can come and catch me cold in my grave."

Love and women made news. When an editor spoke of a specific woman, or of local women in general, he did so within a framework of deferential solicitude. There was always grave danger that semi-literate fathers and suitors would fail to grasp the fine implication of difficult words, and that they might ask the editor to explain his diction at the end of a buggy whip or the point of a shot-gun. In dealing with women in the abstract, editors often adopted a whimsical manner. There were a few long-faced old-timers who still stood before their California cases and composed rambling eulogies attributing strict chastity and piety to all women. The hem of a woman's garment was as sacred to them as were the vessels of the Ark to the Hebrew fathers. Womanly virtue was as unquestioned as the course of the sun. A man who dared speak lightly of woman—any woman—scorned the womb which bore him.

Writing in a flamboyant and gallant style about women was a distinct editorial art. Sometime in its long and romantic past, Kentucky developed a reputation not only for beautiful women, but likewise for women who personified all of man's gentle social aspiration. This tradition was fostered religiously in the southern country press. Often these panegyrics on females became comic indeed. In this modern day when women enjoy emancipation, both social and economic, Colonel Falcon's gallant editorial bow to his neighboring women friends has a rich element of the burlesque in it. "The bluegrass girl," wrote the Colonel, in the Stanford (Kentucky) *Interior Journal,* "is more than equal to a poet's dream. White snow sleeps on her dreamy brow, and down her rounded throat grows whiter till it shames the lace that shields her virgin bosom from the sun. Pink spring with apple blossoms, pelts the lingering drifts that longed to die upon her cheeks, and red summer slumbers with his heart aflame within the curvings of her rounded lips. Clear-eyed and soft of voice, her step is light and springy as the touch the wild roe gives the mountainside when coyly fleeing from her antlered lover, or as that of a dappled fawn on the dewey sward when morning kisses all the earth with tenderness. Roundlimbed, full bosomed, fair in every part, the wind dies dreamily within the meshes of her floating hair, content, swan-like, to sing its last sweet sonnet, at the gateway of her little ear. In every motion is unstinted grace, in every uttered word a melody, down in her limpid eyes a paradise half-guarded only by the long soft lashes which she droops upon her cheeks when looks too bold would penetrate the sanctuary. The sweetheart of a gallant boy, she grows to be a true wife of a noble man and soon has blossomed into motherhood to make the brain and brawn of old Kentucky richer in her progeny."

Southern editors who placed women on pedestals and then trumpeted around them like blind elephants with their pious and hypocritical phrases of gentility were in the minority. This does not mean that there was a lack of interest in the subject by either editor or reader. When news was scarce and there was a need for a human-interest story, a reporter could always stir up a space filler by asking the famous rhetorical question, "What is woman?" "A young lady," answered one such curious philosopher, "is a creature composed of flesh, blood, paint, rings, false hair, old newspapers and plenty of disguised cheek. She never scuffles with pots and pans, but pounds the piano and paints butterflies while her old mother holds down the kitchen and the backache. She don't sit on the front steps with Augustus and talk moonshine until her father comes along and kicks her adored one over the front gate, as every average paragrapher tries to make you believe. No game like that for Mary Ann. She rules the ranch, and while Augustus quotes Tennyson and pulls his moustache, and wishes he could go out for a drink, the old folks have no show north of the dining room. There are some things about a young lady that are hard to understand. We will never know how it is that she can picnic all night and never have strength enough to wash a long pair of thin socks. A young man should marry a young lady when the spirit moves him to quit the sunny vale of bottomless breeches of single life, he should tangle with a single woman—one who is a little stronger on socks and not so all-fired strong on picnics."

Few girls could hold down their mothers' kitchens and the backache at the same time, but the editors loved them just the same. If the numerous accounts of hugging bees which went the rounds of the papers were fairly accurate pictures of country and village life in the South it must not have been altogether as drab as it was pictured in some sober editorials and by social statisticians. A popular feature story listed prices charged at charitable huggings. Girls under sixteen brought fifteen cents for a two-minute hug, and ten cents for a passing squeeze; sixteen to twenty years, fifty cents, with the time severely limited; twenty to twenty-five years, seventy-five cents; another man's wife, one dollar; schoolmarms, forty cents; widows, according to looks, ten cents to three dollars; old maids, three cents apiece, or half a dozen for a nickle, with no time limits. Preachers were not charged; editors were made to pay in advertisements, were not allowed to begin until everybody was through, and could not squeeze anybody except schoolmarms and old maids. Populists were not allowed to hug or squeeze anybody. Sometimes there were follow-up paragraphs of this tomfoolery. It was said that in Alabama a blindfolded victim hugged his wife for one of the more extended and expensive periods and when he discovered his error he demanded a refund of his money. This made the wife angry and she demanded triple payment for her part of the performance.

Perhaps the intimate play-party games helped to feed the constant stream of couples to the marriage altar. Editors were morally bound to write their most flowery pieces about the marriages of the more prominent couples. This became a serious chore because there was just so much which could be said of a wedding ceremony and of the couple involved. Sometimes reporters were at a loss for words which were more original than the hackneyed country-paper adjectives "estimable," "charming," "gracious," "noble," and "accomplished." Wedding reporters could make one of three approaches to their tasks. It was possible to assume a businesslike attitude and report a marriage in the everyday manner of a livestock sale or a political rally, or they could surrender wholeheartedly to the old stereotyped phrases, or they could let their imaginations go wild. It was possible to report the affair in such a manner that it appeared to be as tender and graceful in angelic sweetness as the famous lithograph of "St. Cecilia at the Organ." A characteristic saccharine reportorial outpouring was that of the Fox Trap reporter for the Macon (Mississippi) *Beacon* who wrote, "Ere the stars of the summer night had lighted the dome of the heavens, the guests began to arrive—at 8:45 the seraphiny strains of melody greeted the ear and swelled on the air, awakened on the piano by the beautiful and accomplished Miss Minnie Kincannon, the signal that the hour was at hand for the union of,

> 'Two souls with but a single thought,
> Two hearts that beat as one.'

I gazed on the newly-wedded pair, standing on the threshold of their new life and thought they needed the invocation of an angel charm to rest upon them; starting out under such conspicuous circumstances, could ought but bliss be theirs? The groom appeared as one of nature's noblemen. While the bonny bride was the Helen of Troy, the fair, and surely her sunny smile and winsome ways will ever prove a panacea for all evil, and magic to ward away any shadows that may fall athwart the pathway of her lord." Many of the social reports were boring even to the editors, and they often wished they could find some way to get around what they called the stereotyped "bewhiskered" sentences. One publisher said that he approved of the sentiments expressed in a struggling back-country paper which dismissed its social writing with the bombastic statement that "The ark and his loved are sailing on the lulling waters of a tranquil flood of adoration. We wave at them with an admiring urbanity and infinite affability."

Not all of those who marched to the wedding altars in the New South were Helens of Troy and Norman liege lords in the best Fox Trap, Mississippi, sense of the word. There were far more green bumpkins who were able to make love in their own inimitable way and to secure marriage licenses and take unto themselves "backwoods Marys," who were as unfamiliar with the ways of the world as they were themselves. A couple of this type boarded an Airline Railroad train near Spartanburg to embark upon a marriage journey. The bride spread wide her flowing homemade skirt and seated herself over one of the heating coils of the car. Before the train had gone far, the skirt funneled the heat upward, and the lady became highly excited. This was her first experience with steam heat, and it was none too pleasant. The editor of the Toccoa (Georgia) *News* said she

[65]

jumped into the aisle "with her dry goods at a prominent elevation, and spanking and rubbing herself yelled, 'My Lord, I'm all afire!'" The train was halted and the bride subjected to a detailed examination to determine the location of the flame. Pandemonium reigned in the car, and it was some time before the agitated conductor discovered that his hysterical passenger had been sitting over the radiator.

Southerners of the postwar years loved greenhorn stories. Whether it was reading of a bridal couple who were baffled by the modern system of steam radiation or of a gallant Sut Lovingood in modern dress who was caught without his trousers, these accounts were good reader-interest material. Nearly all of the rural greenhorn stories followed established antebellum patterns, but were applied to local personalities and contemporary situations. One of the best-known stories was that of the two country boys who went courting over the other side of the creek, and while they were gone a trash-moving rain fell and they were unable to go home. This was a trying experience for even the most brazen country boy. There was always danger that he would make an error in etiquette which would bring an immediate end to his love affair. On this particular night one of the boys climbed the peg ladder to the loft bedroom, pulled off his trousers, and was ready to get in bed in his shirttail when curiosity got the better of him, and he was tempted to peep through a knothole in the floor to see what was going on in the girls' room below. A loose plank tilted up and the benighted visitor fell into the middle of the girls' room. He rolled frantically under the bed, screaming, "Bring me my breeches and I'll go home!" His companion was too slow, and his embarrassment was too great for him to linger. He made a dash for the door and headed for the country beyond the swollen creek, trousers or no trousers, for his anxiety was great enough to enable him to swim the Mississippi. It would be impossible to estimate how many thousands of Southerners have sat by their firesides and chuckled at this particular story or one of its more spectacular variations.

Something in the American nature, and in that of the Southerner in particular, has made practical joking a highly regarded pastime. People of the South have joked with one another from the beginning of the region's history. Apparently the more rural a community, the more frequent were the accounts of crass pranks which appeared in the local correspondence to the newspapers. In the dignified old town of Sumter, South Carolina, a rumor was set afloat one Saturday night that there was a dead man lying in the Baptist churchyard. The local marshal cleaned his lantern chimney, assembled a posse, and set forth with most of the town's population, including the local editor, at his heels. The churchyard was searched from front to back, but no body could be found. Then someone happened to think that the body was there all right, but it was well underground. Going back to his office the editor wrote a story about the affair and concluded that "the originator of the huge joke cannot plume himself upon the possession of a vast amount of good judgement."

Actually the attitude toward practical joking was governed largely by the personality of the victim. A common stunt for country jokers was to select a prize patch of corn or cotton near the house of a crotchety old miser and to begin ringing cowbells about in it during the late hours of a dark night. When the swearing farmer staggered out, numbed by sleep, the bell farthest away from him was rung in the nervous manner of a ravenous bell-cow from a dry, bitterweed-ridden pasture who was enjoying life in the midst of a field of succulent young corn. This was kept up until the troubled neighbor gave up in exhaustion, and the bell ringers withdrew from the scene. A week or so later the bedeviled victim discovered from an account published in the local paper that he had been made a goat by his jocular neighbors.

A variation of the bell-ringing trick was for a group of country or small-town boys to take visiting city "dudes" on a watermelon-stealing expedition. They were always careful to walk their victims far enough so as to ensure running them nearly to death coming back. On the way to the imaginary patch of melons, the visitors were told of the fury with which they would be greeted if they were discovered by the owner. The horror of getting shot in a watermelon patch was described realistically enough to ensure a high degree of excitement if any shots were fired. At Stanford, Kentucky, the local wags took the Lehman boys, sons of a Louisville wholesale liquor dealer, on such an adventure. Just before they reached the melon patch they were fired upon and one of the local sons pitched forward screaming that he was shot. The Louisville visitors headed for town, locked themselves in their hotel room, and refused to come out until they were assured that the shooting was all in fun. Early the next morning they caught a train for home, begging the local reporter before they left, "For God's sake don't let the Louisville papers get hold of this!"

There was no end to the human-interest material appearing in the southern weekly papers. It reflects perhaps more intimately and accurately than do long columns of editorializing on political and local issues the true turn of the post–Civil War rural mind. It is one of the reliable sources by which modern students of southern cultural and social history can explore the intellectual processes of the immediate past. Sedate editors, who were wedded to the antebellum philosophy that a newspaper existed as a political or special-interest organ, realized that they could not hope to maintain reader support with their copious diets of profound editorializing. Even conservative publishers frequently relented and presented more ephemeral types of stories to please their subscribers. Readyprint editors, also, had a keen appreciation of this kind of news matter, and they supplied it in great abundance. Perhaps it is safe to say that publicizing the human-interest stories which were a part of the lives of the everyday people of the South was one of the two major reasons for publishing a country paper. As unrelated as much of this material was, it reflected with subtlety a considerable portion of the cultural life of the region. The real meaning of many news stories was to be found in the indirection of their emphasis. Attention was often shifted away from the significant by belittling the major objectives for which the editor was striving.

The most outstanding quality of southern country life between 1865 and 1920 was its extreme provincialism. To a major degree the realm of thought and perception was highly circumscribed by impenetrable barriers of narrow social and economic intercourse. The limited educational and literary opportunities of the region created an unsophisticated appreciation of a simple and provincial style of news reporting. Editorial skill in most of the South was measured not in terms of how well an editor could write long polemic arguments on current issues, but of how well he could condense his news and present it in meaty paragraphs. Most of the editorial pages were composed of brief and spicy paragraphs, phrased in the picturesque language of the region. In short, this method of editorializing put the publisher in the strategic position of speaking most often in witty asides to his readers. Editors keenly appreciated the value of presenting their thoughts and pithy views to their subscribers in a form which was most often called "observations."

III

THE EDITOR
AND THE NEW SOUTH

THE southern country press was essentially a guide to the common man's thinking upon contemporary public issues. Editors assumed full responsibility for presenting community, state, and national problems to their readers in a form that could be readily understood. They interpreted these major issues in a highly editorialized style which most often took cognizance of the indigenous prejudices of the local community. Just as the press dealt with political issues so it did with countless nonpolitical ones which were basic to community welfare.

Any serious consideration of this particular aspect of southern journalism will at the outset raise the question of what the special-interest controls upon the press were. Frequently editors boasted, as did David F. Wallace of the McMinnville (Tennessee) *New Era,* that "The country paper is the honest exponent of unbought opinion and is the only means by which the people of Tennessee can today get unbiased and conscientious truth." Contrary to so positive a statement of chastity, editorial policies were influenced by both selfish economic interests and narrow-minded local public opinion. Many businesses which exploited an uninformed clientele could ill afford to have the searchlight of publicity turned upon their activities. Among the leading advertisers of this character were the myriad patent-medicine companies offering sure cures for every known disease which threatened mankind. From long experience, the fake nostrum sellers learned that any free and intelligent discussion of the validity of their products would do them real harm. Too, there was always the possibility that a muckraking campaign would lead to the passage of legislation which would be embarrassing if not completely destructive. Advertising contracts were cleverly devised in such a way that the medicine companies were able to withdraw this significant source of revenue from a paper without much formal ado upon the infringement of the clause which forbade free discussion of any subject considered detrimental to the best interest of the advertiser.

As a consequence of this type of deterrent influence, scarcely a word can be found in a southern country paper commenting critically upon any one of the hundreds of medicines which they so freely and constantly publicized. Largely because of this fact, practically no regulatory legislation found its way to the state legislative hoppers. When the long-overdue

Pure Food and Drug Act was pending in Congress, little or no news of its course through the legislative routine filtered down to the weeklies. Special Washington reports seem to be devoid of any mention of this issue while it was in the stage of being debated. Likewise, none of the muckraking material which was so virulent elsewhere during the first decade of the present century found its way into either the ready-print pages or the matter which was composed locally. Publishers went on intermixing local news and editorials with medicine advertisements. Grotesque faces of afflicted people, or bloated politicians and neurotic females whose lives had been saved by use of Peruna, beckoned to country readers from advertising columns. Such old Bourbons as Senator M. C. Butler and Governor W. J. Northern proclaimed the virtues of Peruna and other nostrums which promised a certain cure for the most malignant diseases. There was no end to the tonics, elixirs, salves, and female remedies which were advertised. In fact the medicine advertisements were so numerous in many sheets that the papers even seemed to smell of senna leaves, gum opium, and herb-laden alcohol. Ever since the Civil War southern editors have continued to sign contracts with medicine companies. Once many of these called for much "display" advertising located in certain advantageous positions, and for a certain portion of locally composed type matter to be placed in news and editorial columns in the same style as news paragraphs.

As ironical as it may seem in the light of their sorry record with medicine advertisements, country editors accepted full responsibility for stimulating public-spirited movements. "Puffing" home towns and counties was their own particular public service. They were professional braggarts who relished telling the world of the glories of their local communities. At the same time, editors were common scolds who informed officials publicly what the citizens thought of their failures to perform their duties. These published scoldings were most often effective because officials were frightened into action by force of the printed word. Just as recalcitrant officers shrank from public criticism, local rowdies were sometimes brought to bay by pointed editorials which called them down for their misbehavior. Generally it can be said that the local papers were a beneficial influence, if not from the standpoint of vitality of informed editorial writing, then from the wholesome effect of airing many situations which could not stand the light of publicity.

Not all editors were learned men, but most of them were regarded as well-read by their subscribers. In many instances they subscribed to daily papers, read occasional books, and were familiar with some of the popular periodical sources of news and learning. They were among the few men in the towns and hamlets who knew of the bigger world about them, and they accepted the responsibility of interpreting its strange behavior to their readers. Not only were they regarded as viewers of the world, but the guardianship of community morals was often entrusted to them as a matter of locating a safe residual depository. Bands of loudmouthed boys parading through towns at night or hanging around loafing centers were sure to feel the editorial lash. Personal conduct at public meetings was frequently under editorial scrutiny, and was certain to draw public fire if it was not up to a decent standard. When church fathers were dissatisfied with general behavior at religious services they called upon editors to speak to the public for them. Characteristic of this type of editorial lecturing was Colonel W. P. Walton's broad hint in the Stanford (Kentucky) *Interior Journal*. He wrote that "The deacons [?] of the Methodist church desire us to say to the young people who talked during the entire sermon on Wednesday night, that should they again be guilty, their names will be called out in church and a severe reproof given them." On another occasion this editor was somewhat more concerned with the conduct of certain ladies in a congregation than he was with the service of the communion. While looking idly about the congregation he discovered a subject for a pithy editorial observation. A young and lively female communicant was industriously chewing gum, and she had no opportunity to dispose of her cud before the bread was passed. Thus she was caught on the dilemma of removing her gum in public and suffering the opprobrium of her critical neighbors, or of taking the bread in her mouth and swallowing it whole, or of mixing it with the gum. The editor was positive that anyone who chewed gum in church had little religion and little sense, and that his taking the sacrament was the grossest sort of hypocrisy. Many such lapses of good manners and public offenses received editorial attention. To a certain extent southern editors during the latter half of the nineteenth century generally assumed the role of Madame Grundy. They were not so much the inheritors of the strict views of the Puritan Fathers, as they were the authority ex cathedra to publish what they believed to be the prevailing social and moral views of their readers.

Editorial observations and scoldings applied to many subjects. A hole in a poorly constructed board sidewalk in a town was sure to draw fire. Editors have been known to break a leg in one of these places, and the news stories which followed were hardly campaign speeches for the re-election of the responsible town officials. If the boards of aldermen and mayors could not be shamed or lambasted into repairing mudholes or replacing broken planks in sidewalks, then they could be ridiculed into performing their duties. Multiple fires were kindled under officials in three Kentucky towns in 1889. One local editor wrote:

"Noticing our paragraph which stated that a doctor had insisted on the council having the pavement in front of the college here fixed, because it is making the girls bow-legged and twist-ankled, the (Paris) *News* remarks that there are pavements in Paris which make its girls pigeon-toed and bandy-shanked, and the (Winchester) *Sun* says that Winchester has a few which are causing its girls to become 'double-jointed' and knock-kneed; with her limbs, which would otherwise be beautiful as a dream, contorted and misshapen, the coming bluegrass belle will not be able to carry a light for her magnificently formed sister of today."

In towns where there were no pavements, generally there were hogs and weeds. Streets and bypaths were crowded with stray hogs which invoked wrathful editorial comment from one side of the South to the other. These animals persisted in roaming the streets, sleeping in the middle of walkways, rooting up flower beds, gardens and walks, tearing down fences and wallowing slimy puddles around public wells, and playing havoc in general. During the 1880's, 1890's, and the early 1900's this was a favorite topic of editorial criticism. Along with the "pestiferous" hogs were the tall municipal weed patches which snatched ravenously at the last clear foot of walkway. In some towns the weeds grew so tall, and the trails through them became so narrow, that it was impossible for women to sidle along this forest without crushing and staining their clothes. Certainly those maidens who dressed in the wide-flowing skirts of the period found strolling along the average small-town street a tedious pastime. From the numerous accounts which appear in the papers it seems that scores of women were made summer prisoners in their own homes because of an indifference to civic responsibility in keeping the weeds cut back from the walks and the hogs in their pens. Even the Victorian editors realized there was something incongruous in trying to keep alive the moonlight and roses tradition of fair women fashionably dressed in a town full of hogs which on a dark night could not always be distinguished from mudholes and dark shadows. Someone was forever stepping into a bed of sleeping hogs on a dark night and being upset and injured, or horses were being frightened into running away. Southern small-town living which tried to combine the advantages of urban and rural life did not constitute what most publishers meant when they pleaded for people to "live at home."

There was no end to the social and moral obligations of the country editors. They were victims of the narrow and restricted provincial society in which they functioned. An exchange stated the situation with a degree of accuracy when it observed that "to run a newspaper all a fellow has to do is to be able to write poems, discuss the tariff and money questions, umpire a baseball game, report a wedding, saw wood, describe a fire so that readers will shed their wraps, make a dollar do the work of ten, shine at a dance, measure calico, abuse the whiskey habit, test whiskey, subscribe to a charity, go without meals, attack free silver, defend bi-metalism, sneer at snobbery, wear diamonds, invent advertisements, overlook scandal, appraise babies, delight pumpkin raiders, minister to the afflicted, heal the disgruntled, fight to a finish, set type, mold opinions, sweep the office, speak at prayer meetings and stand in with everything and everybody."

Though the above whimsical statement of contradictions somewhat characterized many editors, many more were rugged in their own opinions. Aside from the petty everyday local social irritations and shortcomings there were the broader issues. Some of these took both editor and reader into the difficult field of abstract reasoning. It appears that one question uppermost in the minds of every southern editor for three or four decades was the vital one of the degree of economic and social revolution which had occurred in the region during the Civil War and its immediate aftermath. That fundamental changes had occurred in the South was the most obvious single aspect of the war and Reconstruction. No one had to be told that a new day had dawned, and long before Henry W. Grady made his famous speech before the New England Club in New York, December, 1887, the country editors of his section knew there was a New South.

They held to two views, and sometimes these were in irreconcilable conflict.

Northern political exploitation of the South and the failure of the reconstruction process to erase sectional friction and hatred were one thing in the southern mind, but impersonal northern capitalists interested in developing the region were an altogether different one. Fighting back the petty political despoiler who stole state political offices and ill-gotten economic privilege was a common cause with the southern press. Petty carpetbaggers who drifted South with all their worldly belongings crammed in their famous satchels to cater to Negroes and scalawags were labeled despicable characters. But there was the polite and personable carpetbagger who traveled in a pullman coach, carrying his belongings in a trunk and his credentials in a checkbook, who found a ready and warm welcome wherever he went. This was the northern investor who sought business opportunities which would produce large and steady profits. Country papers almost everywhere in the South campaigned for the investment of outside capital in their states and communities. It angered these editors not at all that northern capital wished to come South. The new economic cry of "On to Richmond!" was as pleasing in 1869 as it had been disconcerting in the closing months of the war. In that year the Abbeville (South Carolina) *Press*

and Banner published a half column of material from
the New York *Herald* which described a journey
made through the South by a party of investors who
had found land to waste, climate of the best sort, and
unlimited productive possibilities.

The fact that so early after the war, and in the
midst of the bitterest days of Reconstruction, editors
were able to see the changing economic situation which
was to characterize the new age is remarkable. They
were able to see the meaning of the industrial age in
its true perspective so far as the South's future was
concerned. A constant task of agitation in most of the
papers was that of securing industry for the South.
This initial campaigning was aimed at acquiring industry for the region as a whole, because most editors
lacked a specific sense of the possibilities of securing
manufacturing plants for local communities. Too,
they were wholly inexperienced in the writing of editorials and news stories which would attract an investment of foreign capital within their territories. Although editors were quick to perceive industrial
changes which were under way and could identify the
forces of the new age, they failed to approach it with
the proper point of view to secure its benefits. It was
here that editors, like most of their readers, best illus-
trated one of the most fundamental weaknesses of
the average southern mind in dealing with the realities
of the industrial age. They knew that both northern
industry and capital were prime necessities, but they

depended upon the northern press and Richard Hath-away Edmonds' *Journal of Commerce* (after 1882, the *Manufacturers' Record*) to supply much of the material which was published. Where northern po-litical opinion was wholly unacceptable, there seems to have been no serious opposition to economic opinion and advice. Numerous articles and editorials were clipped from the sympathetic New York papers, and Edmonds' writings appear to have found a warm reception. In fact, he practically set the economic tone of the southern country press during those years when he was passionately pursuing the idea of industrializ-ing the region.

Country papers portray faithfully the period of economic frustration, 1865–1881. In the latter year even the most isolated four-page "patent sides" jour-nal became aware of the fermentation which was tak-ing place. Economic articles began to appear with more frequency in both original and readyprint mat-ter. Henry W. Grady began to compete with Jefferson Davis and Democratic politicians for news space. Everywhere papers which were published in towns off railroads were campaigning for railroads and hoping eventually to secure factories for their people. Rail-way expansion, 1870–1910, was a leading topic for editorial attention. The approach of a surveying party to a landlocked county-seat town was enough to touch off a spasm of editorial hysteria. Once a line was lo-cated the papers were filled with stories of clearing the right of way, building the road bed, laying steel, and, finally, with an account of that jubilant moment when the first train puffed into town. Hardly had the last echoes of the noisy celebration died away and the first stories been told of what happened to the country hicks who had come to town to see the train, before the papers began persistent drives for northern capital, immigrant labor, and factories.

Editorial observations of the publisher of the Greensboro (Georgia) *Herald* over a period of years were characteristic of the southern country press. In 1874 the editor wrote that Georgia had abundant natural resources, but it needed capital and labor. Freeing the slaves apparently made little difference in the perceptible southern labor supply. Aside from any significant political factors which might have disrupted the normal labor supply there was the grave danger that unreasonably large numbers of Negroes would move away in the migrations to the North and West. White families were showing a restlessness under the uncertainties of postwar conditions, and Texas and the West were beckoning to them. The Georgia editor was certain that a lack of labor prevented a development of natural resources. His state was almost an economic world incapable of being born. Here it must be noted that in these early years, at least, it was not an abundance of cheap labor which was being used by the country press to entice industry South, but rather industry was being sought to aid in increasing the supply of labor. Inducements had to be offered native labor to keep it at home, and to attract desirable foreign immigration.

Seven years later the Greensboro editor was again reviewing Georgia's economic situation. He believed manufacturing possibilities were great. The golden industrial bell, the Atlanta *Constitution,* was pealing forth its clear notes proclaiming the birth of a New South. Henry W. Grady had become the new patron saint of the South of the future, and his fellow editors of the rural press were echoing his enthusiasm. Georgia, said the *Herald,* had mineral resources, water current, forests, and adaptability of every sort. A change was in the making, and it held out bright promise. Slavery had turned the people's thoughts away from a creative and productive economy, except for the growing of raw cotton. People of the antebellum South, it was said, were blind to capital wealth; they disregarded inventive genius and understood little of the manufacturing process. The leisure of the slavery system caused far too much energy to be expended on politics and too little on the development of industry. Men in the New South were no longer dependent upon slavery and the plantation system. No longer were men born to follow the narrow professions of law, the ministry, and medicine. They could now turn to the more material arts; they could move in new grooves, deal with new ideas, and function more freely in an atmosphere where unclouded intellects could perceive more profitable economic returns. "The New South," wrote the Greensboro editor, "will, ere the expiration of another decade, be all the stronger, all the lustier, all the more prosperous and progressive from the very fact of the long repression of her inherent powers; for she is bringing up her great mining and manufacturing reserves. Just at the point when the wants of the world are crying most loudly for them."

Still later, and immediately following the election of 1892, the southern exchanges republished an important article from the New York *Herald*. The *Winston County* (Mississippi) *Journal* carried the full editorial from the New York paper. A monthly review of southern industry, said the *Herald,* showed that "sectional prejudices are stepping into the grave and the bonds of common interests are being tightened." Everywhere southern enterprise and northern capital were working together to develop iron mines, paper mills, cotton mills, and timber resources. It was this union, and not the political one, which was establishing national bonds never again to be broken. Once the nation had contained two antagonistic sections which differed in manners and customs, and between which it was easy to develop jealousies and disaffections. In 1893, however, Massachusetts money was heavily invested in Alabama, and the merchants of the West "are silent partners in ventures scattered from the Potomac to the Gulf. Louisiana and New

York share the fate of new schemes. Business is better than a sponge to clean the old slate and make it ready for a fresh sum in addition. It isn't a new South, it's the South with its eyes open; it is a new North listening to the hum of southern machinery with personal interest in the sale of its products. These things insure the future better than fortifications and a standing army."

Amidst all of the enthusiastic stir to secure northern factories, there was the burning fear that the South would lose its population. Everywhere editors showed the same interest in developing populous communities. Obviously it was not possible to sell papers where there were sparsely populated areas, but the editorial interest went beyond the acquisition of new subscribers. Scarcely a paper published in the region from 1865 to 1900 failed to discuss periodically the subject of emigration. So common was the movement to the West that storekeepers sometimes labeled pages of their bad-debt ledgers "Texas," "Oklahoma," "Kansas," and "Mexico." Editors published Texas stories, some of which were intended to scare people out of moving. The type of letter which Josie Hasty wrote the editor of the Booneville (Mississippi) *Plaindealer* was the kind which editors liked most to publish. Josie had gone to Texas from Mississippi and had been disappointed in what he found. He wrote, "If any of the farmers of Mississippi have any intention of coming to Texas, I would advise them to stay a while longer where they are, for Texas is a rough place. If I was only back there, I would never again sell out and go to Texas. When I get back to Mississippi again, I think I will be willing to make her my home. A person has to work much harder here than there and I say never break up and move here if you can live at all there. . . ."

Northern immigrants, like northern capital, were welcome. Numerous public channels were opened to funnel information to prospective northern settlers that sectional prejudices were relics of the past. C. C. Power, industrial commissioner for the Illinois Central Railroad, wrote in 1893, "While traveling through Mississippi I found a decided impression in favor of encouraging immigration, and the different places were anxious to discover the best means of reaching their object in a satisfactory way. In some cases the towns have offered as high as $500 to any person who will induce twenty-five families to locate, and the ground has been tendered to settlers at rates which will doubtless prove an attraction." The Gulfport (Mississippi) *Seacoast Echo* thought that "To see the flood of prosperity rushing down upon us and not stand up to meet it, is a sin without a pleasure, a thorn without a rose. What we should and must do is to encourage honest working men to settle in the South that it may be prepared to meet and repel the onslaught of the less worthy element that will be sure to follow. . . ."

Excursions were in continuous process, and northern delegations traveled from one southern county to another seeking lands. These visits followed pretty closely the pattern of country-newspaper publication. Out of ninety-six counties in North Carolina, nearly sixty had no papers, and consequently had no way of making known the advantages of their localities. The editor of the Chatham *Record* was of the opinion that counties like Wake, Mecklenburg, Granville, Buncombe, and Orange were prosperous because they had good papers. One of the reasons, he thought, why northern economy had recovered its balance so soon after the Civil War was the fact that the section had at least twenty papers to the South's one. If the southern press of 1881 had existed in 1861 there would have been no war. Thus it is to be inferred that southern editors after 1881 were determined that the region would not be found wanting in the encouragement of participation in the industrial revolution of the latter half of the nineteenth century. If the native labor supply was insufficient to meet the demands of new industry, then the weekly papers would try to stop leaks flowing out of the South, and offer enticements to immigrants to make their homes in the region.

South Carolina papers were awakened to the South's economic plight. The editor of the Edgefield *Monitor* was thoroughly aroused. He admitted that the old system of cotton and slaves was doomed, and

[89]

there was an indication that he was already losing faith in cotton and free tenants. Likewise he admitted that the term "New South" was not a misnomer, but he protested having it crammed down his throat *ad nauseum*. His neighbor, the editor of the Greenville *News,* was less disturbed by terminology. Readily he acknowledged the fact that there was a New South, new in ideas, new in purpose, and new as to its system of life. Southerners, he thought, should cling to the established values of the Old South. They should take great pride in personal honor and courage; they should reverence womanhood, sturdy personal independence, pride of stock, and love of state. These qualities should be combined with a healthy desire for economic gain, and then the South would indeed become a land of prosperity and happiness. Many of the editorials of these decades harked back to antebellum days, as if the editors had a great fear that they were deserting the faith of their fathers. There seemed to be a searching of old personal and economic values in order to determine a new point of departure. Cotton was clearly an economic touchstone in the South, and the primary industrial interest was that of processing raw material close to its source of production. An intelligent search into the question revealed that more than mere production of raw material was involved. As has been said, the editors reasoned in terms of an older southern social and economic tradition. Their first thoughts were of the sanctity of family unity, and cotton mills seemed to offer the best opportunity for keeping families united and for industrializing local communities at the same time. Perhaps their economic thinking was naïve, but it was sincerely directed toward the preservation of the broader aspects of an established southern culture.

Lem Seawright of the Choctaw (Mississippi) *Plaindealer* published a long article in 1893, the basis of which he extracted from the Baltimore *Sun*. The salvation of the South lay in work without restraint or legislative interference. "The true policy of the South," wrote the Mississippi editor, "is to invite both capital and immigration from the North, and to offer every inducement to both to come and take up residence in the South." He assured the northern immigrant he could settle without fear or prejudice. There was no reason for antagonism. "He comes to identify himself with the people and with the soil, and to bring with him his habits of industry, of enterprise and thrift, and ideas and habits of a law abiding citizen." Southern nationalism asserted itself in the editor's mind and he wrote, "He [the Northerner] is a settler infinitely to be preferred to the class of immigrant from abroad which certain European governments are only too glad to dump upon our soil. . . ."

For forty years, agitation for the northern immigrants and northern capital was kept at a fever heat in the press. But politically the South did little to encourage this movement. The southern press had stretched its welcoming arms to Northerners on one page and helped to create a provincially minded and antagonistic system on the other. In 1908 an exchange story was published generally throughout the South in which Richard Hathaway Edmonds of the *Manufacturers' Record* was quoted as saying that southern demagoguery was the dog in the southern industrial manger. Northern capital and northern labor were not so much afraid of social and sectional prejudice as they were of the unpredictable caprices of regional hysteria.

Edmonds spoke from long experience with the *Journal of Commerce,* and later, the *Manufacturers' Record,* in trying to develop an industrial South. Though speaking as he did from mature observation, the Baltimore editor lacked much of explaining the entire southern problem in his interview. Every country editor, however limited his powers of observation, knew that southern economic shortcomings, even beyond the damnable practice of demagoguery, held the region back. Most realistic of all basic community problems to the editor on the ground was the lack of roads. The South was hopelessly in the mud. Where an abundance of undeveloped land was offered as a regional asset, it was at the same time a positive liability. Distances were great, the population was sparse, and capital for road building was nonexistent. Legislators after 1870 were more anxious to save taxpayers a pittance in taxes than they were to build adequate roads. This principle was to characterize a considerable portion of southern social and economic legislation for sixty years. There was little foresight and practicality involved in the economic reasoning of these legislators and their controlling influences.

Almost immediately after the Civil War a few editors began discussing shifting the responsibility for keeping public roads in repair from the shoulders of the taxpayers to that of enforced common labor. Sensible editors saw early that the common-labor system of road maintenance was a failure, and they began advocating the more responsible contract method. In 1870 the publisher of the Selma (Alabama) *Southern Argus* said that the dirt roads leading out of that town were impassable and that there was little or no hope that they would be improved. He advocated letting the construction and maintenance of roads on contract, and then setting up toll gates to collect funds to maintain them.

Characteristic of the southern road laws was that of South Carolina which was abstracted by John S. Werner in 1881 for the readers of his Keowee *Courier*. The act of 1875 provided for construction of main roads thirty feet wide, and for all others to be twenty feet in width. In 1879 a second act provided for overseers who were empowered to use all timber and stone found along the right of way, except rail timber, shade trees, and stone which had to be taken from cultivated fields. Every able-bodied man from sixteen to fifty years, except ministers, schoolteachers, school trustees, and members of boards of assessors, was liable for fifteen days' work a year, or the payment of a dollar a day to hire a substitute. A system of overseers was established with the responsibility for warning men out to work on the roads, and to see that the highways were kept in passable condition. Actually overseers adopted the practice of working the roads just before each session of the grand jury, thus keeping one technical jump ahead of the law but seldom maintaining passable roads.

When an editor anywhere in the South wished to vent his wrath on someone he could always single out the road overseers and heap coals of criticism on their heads. Nowhere were the roads up to a decent standard. Sidney Lewis of the Sparta (Georgia) *Ishmaelite* argued incessantly for new road laws. Wisely he contended that road construction and maintenance were a direct responsibility of the state government and not of the individual citizen. It was ridiculous he thought to include boys so young as sixteen and to exempt men over fifty. Although in a great majority of cases young men did little or no hauling over the roads, they were liable for fifteen days of labor each year. Scores of men over fifty years of age had dozens of teams using the roads daily and were in no way liable for their upkeep and construction. Occasionally an editor like that of the Abbeville (South Carolina)

Press and Banner objected to the proposed contract system. He fell back upon the antiquated argument that public benefits were individual responsibilities. If a man wished to use the roads or to send his children to school then let him work to supply them and not tax the public at large. However, this was the petty contention of an insignificant reactionary minority.

On top of the old-line editorial argument concerning the upkeep of roads, was the new one for so-called "good roads." The concept of good roads was a much broader one than that involved in the ineffective road laws of the post-Reconstruction era. Grand-jury presentments generally condemned the old system, and newspaper publicity was unfavorable from the beginning. In agitating for good roads, southern country editors grappled with one of the most deterrent forces in their local communities. Soon after the war they were able to sense the effect of isolation. Always, to the editors, communication and education were vital if their papers were to succeed, or if their editorializing was to take effect with an informed constituency. In agitating for good roads the country press had literally to batter aside the ancient concepts that public benefits were individual responsibilities and that men with money had the right to make the choice of their own participation. In many sections of the South editors could take credit for breaking down for the first time the barriers of strangling isolation and antisocial individualism in the campaign for good roads. Without a doubt the influence of the press was great. Some notion of the large world which lay beyond, but contiguous to the local community, was revealed in both editorials and advertisements. As the era of industrialization of the late nineteenth and early twentieth centuries began to make its influence felt, the editorial tasks grew lighter.

Breaking down the barrier of isolation was a major editorial responsibility, but so was that of lowering the alarming rate of illiteracy. Clearly, before the social and economic level of a southern community could be raised materially it was necessary to elevate the level of education. In 1870 W. L. Perry's Americus (Georgia) *Tri-Weekly Republican,* flaunting at its masthead "Liberty, Justice, White Supremacy," voiced a positive opinion in favor of public education. He welcomed the public free school and hoped that it would be free of politics. Perry was certain that schools for the common man had been too long neglected in the South. Too much energy had been expended in other fields, and too large a percentage of mature Georgians were hopelessly illiterate. Georgia and the South needed nothing so much as universal education. "We don't know," wrote this editor in 1870, "but what we would favor a law forcing every parent to send their children to school for a specific term of years." It was agreed that a good common-school system would probably remove the excuse for

poverty. Voters were asked to nominate only candidates for office who favored an adequate system of
schools.

Five years later W. P. Walton gave his local correspondent, "Rienzi," considerable space in which to
deal with the subject of education. Farmers in Bluegrass Kentucky appeared to be trying to slam the door
of opportunity on the schools. "It seems difficult for
the people of Lincoln [County] to become fully aware
that this great and busy world is moving onward; that,
with the exception of improving farming implements,
the blood of jackasses, cattle, horses, and liberally
taxing the people to construct a pike by every princely
bluegrass farmer's door, she is lagging far behind. . . ."

Educational responsibilities said the Dayton (Tennessee) *Weekly Leader* could be summed up in the
Jeffersonian philosophy that "If a nation expects to
be ignorant and free in a state of civilization it expects
what never was and never will be." Various informed
groups admitted that the South's greatest need was
adequate education, but it was impossible to see sufficient aid coming from within the section itself. Many
of the papers favored the idea of federal aid, and
during the decade 1880–1890, when the Blair Bill
was pending, a considerable amount of space was
given to its discussion. So long as this bill was kept on
a basis of federal support for common schools it received a favorable press in the South, but the moment

Senator M. C. Butler of South Carolina and Congressman John Tyler Morgan of Alabama, in a narrow demagogic way, injected the race issue into discussion of the bill it became anathema to many papers. So poisonous, in fact, was the race issue in the Blair proposal that editors who had otherwise been ardent in support of improved schools lost sight of the proposed legislation's main objective in their rabid opposition to social equality. Lewis M. Grist, of the Yorkville (South Carolina) *Enquirer,* believed the Blair Bill a step in the right direction. He felt that the approximately $450,000 which would come to each of eight southern states would go far toward lowering the barrier of ignorance. Of course the bill would result in great benefit to Negro children, but Grist could see no justifiable reason why white children should be penalized by rejecting federal aid on such a ground.

Editors dealt generally with school finances. Every year the same types of reports were made on both the local and state systems. Occasionally editorials commented upon the ridiculously low salaries paid teachers. In Newberry County, South Carolina, a movement was on foot in 1887 to reduce teachers' pay to ten and fifteen dollars per month. The editor of the Winnsboro *News and Herald,* published in the neighboring county of Fairfield, condemned such an idea as an act of the grossest hypocrisy. This was a common attitude throughout the South. Everywhere the press recognized that schools would continue to be taught by inferior teachers until their economic lot was improved. At the same time that the country journals wrestled with the problem of organizing satisfactory local school systems, they took editorial swings at those shortsighted and selfish interests which wished to support schools purely on the basis of individual responsibility. A series of editorial comments appearing in the Paulding (Georgia) *New Era* indicated that if such an idea prevailed there would be no publicly supported institutions, and every man would be resolved "into a selfish two-legged brute."

Southern education involved more than merely local attitudes. There was a close kinship in many respects between attitudes toward an adequate school system and the importation of industry. In 1902, Editor Shipp of the Greensboro (Georgia) *Herald* reminded his patrons that the visit of the Ogden Committee to the South was indicative that the region was still a subject of missionary concern on the outside. "The South," he wrote, "has everything, yet it sits like Lazarus at the rich man's table." He reviewed in graphic terms the section's troubles. It had good land and a temperate climate, but class and discriminatory legislation had proved expensive. On the other hand, pensions for northern soldiers were burdensome; northern philanthropists had been enriched in the South and rightfully they owed it a financial return. But withal, it was no time to bemoan the region's fate. Schools and industry held the key to future happiness. Until the South's economic resources were developed, northern capital would continue to exploit southern industry, and northern philanthropy would have to continue to contribute to educating its children.

The first three decades of the twentieth century saw the realization of many press predictions. Following almost identically the same pattern of agitation for good roads there were simultaneous campaigns for better schools. Consolidation of rural schools into larger units, and the organization of adequate high schools received a tremendous amount of space in the papers. Agricultural and mechanical colleges and their attendant agricultural experiment stations were organized in the states, and arguments for and against them appeared in the weeklies. These arguments were as indicative of the fear and uncertainty which the region was experiencing as they were of the improvement of educational facilities. Actually the South was departing, belatedly, from a frontier condition. The more progressive examples of other sections of the Union were forcing it to move faster than a large portion of the population could make adjustments to new ideas.

Schools were social necessities. A majority of the editors were anxious to support them and were gratified when they succeeded, but there were other social institutions which received editorial attention. There has ever been competition in the South between the school system and those agencies which minister to the socially dependent and the criminal. Convict labor was a burning issue everywhere. Apparently no southern state had gone beyond the idea that a man who was convicted of a crime against society lost control of his life and limb. Perhaps the press gave no more attention to any other social maladjustment than it did to the public failure to care properly for convict labor. During the latter decades of the nineteenth century and the first decade of the present one, a tremendous amount of publicity was given this issue by the country press. The editor of the Troy (Alabama) *Messenger* spoke critically of both the management of the convicts and the Montgomery *Advertiser* because the *Advertiser* had failed to take a positive course in the Alabama convict muddle. "We might just as well have watched a Chinese praying machine," wrote the Troy editor. Colonel John Bankhead had inspected the prisoners' backs and found them in horrible condition. The ghastly effects of the lash had caused the shirts to stick to their bodies, and they were otherwise abused. The common approach to this issue was to use extreme examples of horror which indicated that once a man was convicted and sent to a convict camp he faced punishment more horrible than death itself.

For years politicians, under the influence of self-seeking interests which wished to lease this type of slave labor, dawdled with the convict question. There was a movement in every state in the South to reconstruct the whole penal program and to employ the criminal in humane but noncompetitive work which would be profitable to society. A major question in the eyes of the Elberton (Georgia) *New South* was what Georgia should do with 1,200 to 1,300 convicts. Its editor did not want the state to go to the expense of constructing an adequate penitentiary, and anyway he thought working in the open air was better for the prisoners. They should be employed in such a way as not to compete with honest labor, but to yield a profit. Roads needed building, and there was other public work which could be performed. He thought the legislature should use the convicts in such a way as to create advantages which would attract immigrants. This is a general review of the leading points at issue which were brought to light so many times in the weekly papers. Most editors wished to destroy the lease system, but at the same time they wished to reduce public expenses for care of prisoners, and did not want them to compete with private labor.

Criminality in the South was a greater issue than was indicated in the heated discussions of convict labor. There was the whole broad field of law enforcement and the courts which involved matters of both public demeanor and race relationships. Carrying pistols and drinking liquor were ever productive of editorials pleading for law and order.

The New South was not a land of peace and order. War with its tribulations and reckless bloodshed had left its deep and smarting scar. Out of this social maladjustment came a wave of wanton criminality which threatened social safety and any possibility of racial harmony. News stories of the hundreds of bloodcurdling accidents with guns indicated the degree to which ownership of arms was prevalent, and how much they were admired and valued by rural people. There was truth in the contention of the Fayette (Mississippi) *Chronicle* when it commented upon a recent law passed by the Mississippi legislature which restricted sale of toy pistols and prescribed a fine of $50 to $60 in case of the law's violation. No mention was made of the "real thing" said the editor. He believed that "homicidal records of the courts can only be abolished with abolition of pistols. Pistols are made to take human law in hand. The man who makes an arsenal of his hip pocket contemplates possible difficulty and homicide. A pistol gives the bully the drop, and the coward the power of life and death." Actually the editor believed the legislature was "toying with a momentous situation."

Across the line in Alabama editors cried out against the pistol. The Bingtown *Bugle* was certain that there was a close correlation between pistol toting and the state's high homicidal rate. Editors asked for a fine of not less than $100, and even more drastic punishment. There was general agreement with the sentiment expressed by the Indianola (Mississippi) *Enterprise* that "the man who is forever toting a pistol, so as to be handy when he fills his hide with cheap booze, is the veriest type of a coward, but at the same time a dangerous being, and should, when apprehended, be given the full limit of the law. It is not safe for respectable people to walk the streets where pistol toters are allowed to roam at large."

Love of guns because of a sporting instinct is hardly sufficient reason to explain the general pattern of violence which prevailed in the South. Perhaps there was a tradition of frontier rowdiness in the section, but this is not a fully competent explanation of the lack of respect for personal safety. Reconstruction had only added fuel to the dangerous flames of violence which the war had started. During this period there was developed an unbridled spirit of individualistic self-defense which was contributory to a poorly ordered domestic peace. Whatever the causes, the problems of law enforcement were so varied and complex that no certain general statement will suffice to explain them. There was a mistrust of the courts, a fear of duplicity on the part of peace officers, a certainty of the wiles of lawyers, and a lack of faith in the jury system. It may even be contended that there was a sadistic tinge to the southern nature, but this could have been true only within a limited scope of criminal action.

Violence in many forms prevailed. Murder, arson,

rape, armed robbery, and mutilation were frequently mentioned in the papers. But of all these, rape and manslaughter appear to have been the most highly publicized of capital offenses. Country papers were horrendous chronicles of lynching bees which followed the commission of many crimes. In the dark days of the 1870's, when southern civilization was at its lowest state of bewilderment and frustration, there appeared the opening chapters of a long and revolting story of rapine and lynching. These nearly always involved the more complex issue of racial friction, and news stories were slanted with this angle. The young daughter of Asa Fortson of Oglethorpe, Georgia, was assaulted in a heartless manner, and there followed a gruesome account of the lynching of the brute who had perpetrated the crime. "We are not in favor of lynch law as a general thing," wrote the editor of the Oglethorpe *Echo*, "but we think that every case of rape should be met with instant death from the people. It will learn the blacks a lesson that naught else will—particularly where the case is of such an aggravating character as the one to which allusion is made above. Never in our lives, have we seen so many accounts of rape of Negroes upon white ladies as in the past few weeks. Every paper is filled with accounts of them. Let our people make a determination to hang *on the spot,* everyone caught in the act, and we guarantee it will put a quietus on it when nothing else will."

The *Echo*'s plea was representative of the extreme point of view. As the South grew away from the '70's and '80's there crept into the press a sobering note. Editors became more courageous in supporting what they conceived to be the sanctity of the law and the courts. A few rabid editors like J. D. Peacock of the *North Mississippi Herald* let their judgment fly to the wind. He wrote: "I advocate it [lynch law] from the housetop in season and out of season, and I have no sympathy for efforts on the part of any officer to save a white or black brute from certain, sure and a terrible death. I don't think it should be honored with a jury. I believe it a crime to tax the people for the purpose of a trial in court." Soberer editors were of the opinion that lynching only accomplished the depravity of a community. A victim suffered a few moments and he was gone, but in the manner of his going he left behind a shocked people who were to be victims of a social neurosis for years to come. There was no denying the existence of crime and the technical delays of the courts. County jails were flimsy structures, and jail deliveries were noted frequently in the press. A lack of evidence to convict known criminals, and mistrials brought about by the crafty manipulations of evidence by lawyers: these things, plus an inborn fear of the dangers lurking in isolated communities, contributed to a desire to mete out speedy punishment for capital crimes. But always there was the question

[106]

of determining guilt and innocence, and of where the line should be drawn between capital and secondary crimes. This point was well taken in many editorials. At the beginning of the present century the editor of the Linden (Alabama) *Reporter* expressed the opinion that sentiment against lynching was growing. Governor W. D. Jelks, a former country editor, and the Alabama circuit judges were using their influence to ensure fair trials. Sheriffs were showing more courage, and were ceasing to run all over a state with prisoners in search of safe jails away from the mobs. The state militia was rapidly becoming a block to the illicit use of the rope, the pistol, and the firebrand.

In North and South Carolina, laws were passed in the 1890's to check mob rule. North Carolina stripped its courts of many of the technicalities which had impeded the process of speedy trials for criminal-assault cases. In South Carolina, communities were held liable by constitutional amendment for permitting the occurrence of lynchings. Fines were levied against counties, and, if they refused to pay, they were required to deliver the lynchers. The editor of the Fayette (Mississippi) *Chronicle* wrote, "We are much mistaken if it does not stop lynching in the Palmetto State." Perhaps it is not possible to say what positive role the sane editor played in the crusade against mob rule, but certainly his editorials pleading for the chance to permit the courts to try cases on their merits and free from inflamed emotions bore fruit. Lynching has not yet been completely stamped out, but it has shown a marked decline in the last three decades. In the process of accomplishing this end it is at once noticeable that there is less evidence of a fear complex expressed in the weekly editorials, and more reverence for the courts and law. Too, there has disappeared from the papers the constant stream of accounts of accidents caused by careless handling of pistols and shotguns. Even Sidney Lewis of the Sparta *Ishmaelite,* who lived through a period when more than three hundred lynchings occurred in Georgia, was able to write in 1906, *"The Clansman* is coming South again with Dixon, the fanatic still shaking the red flag. The play will do infinite harm to our conditions in Georgia. There was a time when it would have been appropriate. The play possesses no remarkable literature, no scenic qualities and let us hope this trip will be the last."

There was a constant flow of other matters of major importance which came weekly to the country editor's attention. He preached in literally thousands of editorials against the unfortunate single-crop system which beset the southern farmer. He saw the agrarian portion of the population being made debtors and slaves to outside meat packers, fertilizer trusts, merchants, speculators, and bankers. He opened wide his columns to long and tedious discussions of the merits and demerits of the open and closed range. At times he was prophetically mindful of the necessity for conservation of natural resources. He was ever dutiful to the Lost Cause, but at the same time he recorded with faithfulness a running story of the road back to reunion. By 1898 and the outbreak of the war with Spain, the moderate editor, out of sentimentality, was waving the Confederate flag with one hand and keeping time with the other to the stirring martial strains of John Philip Sousa's *Stars and Stripes Forever.*

In a final analysis, the New South, intellectually at least, may be regarded as a series of intimately related social and economic problems. This fact made editing a country paper a serious responsibility. Thousands of subscribers never read any other printed matter except the Bible, and their sense of the world about them was derived almost entirely from the weekly paper. On the whole, country editors, within their limitations of education and training, assumed a progressive point of view toward the future of their region. Their more thoughtful editorials, and especially, slanted news stories, reflected an innate sense of justice and a genuine desire to improve the lot of the common man. Sometimes the editors approached the solution of public issues with narrow political and provincial concepts. When they did, their prejudices showed through their reasoning in the same ungraceful manner that ribs of exhausted cotton mules on neighboring farms were exposed to view at laying-by time.

Because editors worked indoors, wore collars and ties everyday, and were confined to the towns, many agrarian readers were convinced that they were impractical and unacquainted with the real problems of men who labored with their hands. Because of this foolish point of view, many publishers met with rebuffs and were often tempted to give up their fight for progress. This highly individualistic agrarian philosophy of most of the rural New South made extremely difficult the job of editorializing for a better-ordered community, importation of new capital and industries, breaking the bonds of constrictive isolation, improving educational facilities, and correcting major social problems. It took real courage to oppose small-town and rural bigotry and special interests, but it was an even more trying task to destroy the rigidity of the southern provincial mind. The lack of perspective and tractability of thought on the part of fully 90 per cent of the rural subscribers forced editors to move slowly in setting forth new ideas. In fact, the fundamental influence of the country paper is not to be measured in terms of large accomplishments which were made within short periods of time. Rather, the effect of this type of journalism is to be determined in terms of the slow and patient way in which society was brought to make changes of its own accord. There was ever a feeling on the part of a large portion of the southern population that social and economic betterment at any time during the period 1865–1918 was too expensive. Too, the ever-present fear of the influence of the North, of infidelity to the southern tradition, of the race issue, of the trusts, of the Republican party, and of financial failure at home caused a reluctance to change the *status quo*. But whatever progress resulted, and whatever attitude the southern common man adopted toward his community responsibilities as a citizen in a democratic society, he was influenced in that attitude by the country paper. It brought the issues home to him in the simple and clear everyday language of a generally trustworthy neighbor.